BIBLE KEY WORDS

VII. BASILEIA

MANUALS FROM KITTEL

BIBLE KEY WORDS
FROM GERHARD KITTEL'S
THEOLOGISCHES WÖRTERBUCH
ZUM NEUEN TESTAMENT

———

BASILEIA

BY

K. L. SCHMIDT
H. KLEINKNECHT
K. G. KUHN, AND
GERHARD VON RAD

ADAM & CHARLES BLACK
LONDON

THIS EDITION FIRST PUBLISHED 1957
BY A. AND C. BLACK LIMITED
4, 5 AND 6 SOHO SQUARE LONDON W. I

Translated from the German, with
additional notes, by H. P. Kingdon

PRINTED IN GREAT BRITAIN
AT THE UNIVERSITY PRESS ABERDEEN

PREFACE

THE chief aim of this volume—which is the seventh in this series of English translations of Kittel's famous New Testament *Wörterbuch*—is to clarify the meaning of the often enigmatic phrase " kingdom of God " in the New Testament. The tradition so far followed by my distinguished and much-lamented predecessor, the late Professor J. R. Coates, has been to transliterate Hebrew and Aramaic words, but to leave Greek words occurring in the German text in their original lettering. I have followed his example in the case of Hebrew and Aramaic words, and also in the case of Greek quotations mainly of interest to experts in that language ; but in the belief that this volume will be of special value also to many pastors and students who do not easily read Greek in the original but have a nodding acquaintance with many of the terms most common in the New Testament, I have transliterated many Greek, as well as all Hebrew, words into English letters, and occasionally translated them into English, and still more rarely both ; the presence of transliteration is always indicated by the use of italics, and where these are used for Hebrew words I have distinguished Greek words by leaving them in the original lettering. It seemed best, however, not to adhere to any very rigid rule in other cases ; thus a Greek word that occurs especially often has occasionally been transliterated, occasionally not. This is partly for aesthetic reasons, but it may incidentally give practice to those who do not read Greek easily.

These considerations have particularly influenced me in the New Testament section, where students whose knowledge of Greek is so slight that they stand in special need of such studies as this in their preparation of sermons and lessons will specially look for guidance in this so central subject. Here, too, the German text usually has the traditional translation " Reich " for *basileia*, and I have mostly translated it " Kingdom " ; but those who use mainly this part of the book are asked to remember that it has been earlier established that " Herrschaft "—dominion or sovereignty (cf. p. 32 ad. fin.) is the root meaning of the word ; but to reiterate this too much in the most familiar texts might seem pedantic. In view of this, however, the word *Basileia* has been left as the title of the book ; the German original is at the same time on *basileūs*, and other cognate words.

The few additions I have ventured to make to the text or notes are always in square brackets ; a very few of the notes in the original have been abbreviated or omitted. So also with some books in the German Bibliography—where it is also pointed out that almost all books dealing with the origins of Christianity are relevant to the theme.

Since the publication of the first volume of the *Wörterbuch* in 1932-3, there has been much discussion among New Testament scholars as to the extent to which the " last things " (*ta eschata*) mentioned in the Gospels may be said to have been already realised in the earthly life of Jesus—how far " eschatology " (a word more honoured by use than by precise definition) has been " realised ". Professor J. Jeremias, on page 157 of the English translation of his great book on the *Parables of Jesus*, sums it up by saying that " they are all full of ' the secret of the Kingdom of God ' (Mk. iv, 11) that is to say, the recognition of ' an eschatology that is in process of realisation ' ", and he adds a footnote saying that this formulation has the agreement in principle of Professor C. H. Dodd—who first used the phrase ' realised eschatology '. I have added a footnote on page 43 to call attention to this now widely accepted modification of earlier interpretations. But we may do well to remember that it is often a *telos*, rather than an *eschaton*—or any ' -ology '—that is referred to as being realised in the New Testament.

Another field of recent deepening of our understanding of the New Testament is the greater realisation of the part played by extreme Jewish nationalism—what came to be called zealotry [1]— from 50 B.C. to A.D. 73, and its probable link with the " false Christs " and brigands mentioned in Josephus and the Gospels, against whom Jesus warned His disciples. The prevalence of their contaminating teaching about the Messiah and Kingdom— which led to the destruction of the Temple, as foretold by Jesus— is perhaps a main reason for the absence of the term *basileia* in Josephus,[2] who also mentions Messiahship with reluctance, and also for the disassociation of the term *malkûth* from Messiah in Rabbinic Judaism.[3] These insights, and the Dead Sea Scrolls,

---

[1] E.g. Oscar Cullmann, *The State in the New Testament* (Eng. tr. 1957).

[2] See p. 26, infra.

[3] See p. 20f. Chronologically this chapter on Rabbinic Judaism should come last in the book, as its sources were not written down till A.D. 200 and may well have been as much influenced by the Gospel teaching as *vice versa* ; but they are of course of help in determining the meaning of Gospel terms, and are therefore treated first.

provide new material for the not yet published Kittel articles on *Christos* and *Pseudochristoi*.

For the rest, although the statement (p. 47) that " whoever concentrates wholly upon ethics centres his logic upon the single individual " may seem to smack too much of a mode of thought specially characteristic of German protestantism in the beginning of the Nazi era (though certainly not of the Nazis) it is my hope that this volume will not only correct Anglo-Saxon misunderstandings of German evangelical scholarship but prove a permanent enrichment to our own.

Of the German authors of this article, Professor K. L. Schmidt, of whose career and publications a summary is given in his companion volume in this series on *The Church*, died on 10th January, 1956. The present editor of the Wörterbuch, Professor G. Friedrich, now of Erlangen, tells me that Professor Kleinknecht is at Münster, Professor Kuhn and Professor von Rad at Heidelberg.

H. P. KINGDON

CONTENTS

BIBLIOGRAPHY

I. GREEK USAGE

PAULY-W., III (1899), s.v. ' Basileus '
E. LOHMEYER : *Christuskult und Kaiserkult* (1919), pp. 11 ff., etc.
A. DEISSMANN : *Licht vom Osten*, pp. 310 f.
ARISTOTLE : *Politics* III, 14, p. 1284b, 35 ff.

II. O.T. USAGE

H. GRESSMANN : *Der Messias* (1929).
E. SELLIN : *Die israelitische-jüdische Heilandserwartung* (1909) ; *Der alttestamentliche Prophetismus* (1912).
S. MOWINCKEL : *Psalmenstudien* II: *Das Thronbesteigungsfest Jahwes und der Ursprung der Eschatologie* (1922).
A. VON GALL : *Basileia tou theou* (1926).
R. KITTEL : *Die hellenistische Mysterienreligion und das A.T.* (1924).
BOUSSET-GRESSMANN : *Die Religion des Judentums im Späthellenistischen Zeitalter* (3rd edn. 1926).

III. RABBINIC LITERATURE

G. DALMAN : *Worte Jesu*, i, pp. 75-119 (cf. 2nd edn. 1930, 375, ff.) [Eng. translation, 1902].
STRACK und BILLERBECK : *Kommentar zum N.T. aus Talmud und Midrasch* (1921), i, pp. 172-184 and *passim*.
G. F. MOORE : *Judaism* (1927, ff.), I, 401, 432, ff. ; II, 346 f., 371-5.

V. NEW TESTAMENT

See above. Besides this we only add the latest literature on *basileia* in the N.T. owing to the immense amount that has been written, including the references to the subject in all comprehensive works on primitive Christianity ; cf. P. Feine, *Theologie des N.T.* (1931), 73 ff. (he gives a good bibliography); also K. L. Schmidt, *Jesus Christus* in RGG (2), iii, 110-51. For further detailed research see W. Mundle : *Reich Gottes* RGG (2), iv, pp. 1817-22. For discussions see the Report on the first British-German Theologians' Conference in Canterbury : *Das Wesen des Reiches Gottes und seine Beziehung zur menschlichen Gesellschaft* (Theologische Blätter, vi (1927), pp. 113 ff. (N.T. contributions by C. H. Dodd, E. C. Hoskyns, G. Kittel, A. E. J.

Rawlinson, K. L. Schmidt). [The English edition was entitled *Mysterium Christi.*]

German monographs :

G. HOLSTEIN : *Die Grundlagen des ev Kirchenrechts* (1928), 5 ff.

W. MICHAELIS : *Täufer, Jesus, Urgemeinde, die Predigt Jesu vom Reiche Gottes vor und nach Pfingsten* (1928).

J. KÖSTER : *Die Idee der Kirche beim Apostel Paulus* (1928).

G. GLOEGE : *Reich Gottes und Kirche im N.T.* (1929).

H. E. WEBER : " *Eschatologie* " *und* " *Mystik* " *im N.T.* (1930).

H. D. WENDLAND: *Die Eschatologie des Reiches Gottes bei Jesus* (1931).

OTHER LITERATURE

[E. F. SCOTT : *The Kingdom of God* (1931).

T. W. MANSON : *The Teaching of Jesus* (1931).

C. H. DODD : *The Parables of the Kingdom* (1935).

E. T. GUIGNEBERT : *The Jewish World in the Time of Jesus* (1939).

C. J. CADOUX : *The Historic Mission of Jesus* (1941)—with bibliography.

R. OTTO : *The Kingdom of God and the Son of Man* (revised 1943).

S. H. HOOKE : *The Kingdom of God* (1949).

T. W. MANSON : *The Sayings of Jesus* (1950).

T. W. MANSON : *The Servant-Messiah* (1953).

R. H. FULLER : *The Mission and Achievement of Jesus* (1954).

J. JEREMIAS : *The Parables of Jesus* (1954).]

Square brackets, here and elsewhere, indicate additions by the translator.

ABBREVIATIONS

Ditt. Or.   W. Dittenberger, Orientis Graecae Inscriptiones (1902 ff.).

Ditt. Syll.   W. Dittenberger, Sylloge Inscriptionum Graecarum (3rd edn. 1915 ff.).

I.G.   Inscriptiones Graecae (Preussische Akademie 1873 ff.).

Moore   G. F. Moore, Judaism (1927 ff.).

Pauly-W.   Pauly-Wissowa, Realencyclopedie der klassischen Altertumswissenschaften (1892 ff.).

RGG.   Die Religion in Geschichte und Gegenwart (2nd edn. 1927 ff.).

S-B.   H. L. Strack und P. Billerbeck, Kommentar zum N.T. aus Talmud und Midrasch (1922 ff.).

Z.A.W.   Zeitschrift für die alttestamentliche Wissenschaft (1881 ff.).

Z.N.W.   Zeitschrift für die neutestamentliche Wissenschaft (1900 ff.).

I. GREEK USAGE

THE word *basileūs* [1] denotes the king as the legal, and usually hereditary priestly ruler of the people in a good sense. In later political practice and theory it is contrasted with the *turannos* as usurper. [2] In the well known passage in the *Odyssey* XIX, 108 ff., Homer gives a legendary picture and a paean of the good king and the blessings attendant upon his reign. The justice or injustice of a *basileūs* shows its results in the life of his people, who share in his penances or prosperity. The king's power is traced back to Zeus (*Iliad* II, 197) a relationship characterised by the common adjective *diotrephes* (*Iliad* II, 196, etc.) " fostered by Zeus ". In Hesiod, where the King is conceived of essentially as a figure of knightly chivalry, we find a standard developed doctrine of kingly wisdom. Kings as well as bards are inspired by the Muses—Kalliope βασιλεῦσιν ἅμ' αἰδοίοισιν ὀπηδεῖ (*Theogony* 80). To speak with certitude (ἀσφαλέως ἀγορεύειν 86)—that is the ἱερὴ δόσις of the Muses to kings. This early Greek ideal of the king gives birth to the philosophical discussion of the ideal king in Plato's *Politicus:* the knowledge of the " ideas " is the kingly art, and its possessor the kingly man (*Politicus* 292 e; cf. the famous sentence Plato, *Republic* V, 473d: ἐὰν μὴ . . . ἢ οἱ φιλόσοφοι βασιλεύσωσιν ἐν ταῖς πόλεσιν ἢ οἱ βασιλεῖς τε νῦν λεγόμενοι

[1] It is generally accepted that *basileūs* is borrowed from the pre-Greek " Aegaean " language (Debrunner, *Real-lexikon für Vorgeschichte* IV, 2 (1926), p. 526). See also attempts at its earlier etymology in Pauly-W., op. cit. 55 f.

[2] Cf. Aristotle, *Nicomachean Ethics* VIII, 12, p. 1160 b 3 and Suidas' definition s.v. Pindar speaks of the priest as *basileūs, Olympian Odes* I, 23, *Pythian Odes* 3, 70, as *turannos, Pythian Odes* 3, 85.

καὶ δυνάσται φιλοσοφήσωσι γνησίως . . . οὐκ ἔστι κακῶν
παῦλα . . . ταῖς πόλεσι, δοκῶ δ᾽ οὐδὲ τῷ ἀνθρωπίνῳ γένει . . .)
Thus Plato, reacting against a long development, is at
the same time precursor of Hellenism with its quite
new concept of the king. It developed the idea of the
" Benefactor King " [1] who moves god-like over the
heads of men, and tends them like a shepherd his sheep.
He knows no law except the personal law of his will,
which is not subject to any communal constitution:
and his will is the norm not only of a definite country
or state but of everything. The being and the office
of the king can be summed up by saying that he is
benefactor to the entire world.[2] From these philosophical ideas of the fourth century developed, under
the influence of the towering figure of Alexander the
Great, the hellenistic " divine kingship ". The primitive Greek faith in the divinity of the politically
creative personality fused in Hellenism with the special
God-king conceptions of different oriental cultures.
Thus *basileūs* is used for the hellenistic God-king, the
basileūs megas or later occasionally the *basileūs basileōn*,
as e.g. Antiochus I of Commagene: *basileūs megas
Antiochos theos*. . . . Ditt. Or. 383, 1, as also the Roman
Caesars.[3] His *basileia* is an *anupeuthunos archē* (Suidas
s.v.).

[1] *Euergetēs* is a specially popular and significant eponym of the
hellenistic kings, as e.g. Antigonus and Demetrius were hailed as
theoi sōtēres kai euergetai.

[2] E. Lohmeyer, op. cit. p. 12. Cf. Plato, *Politicus* 267 d, 275 b,
Aristotle, *Politics* III, 13, p. 1284 a 13—the picture of the ideal ruler
who cannot be placed beneath the *nomoi* because he is himself *nomos*;
and the ideal *pambasileia*—III, 10, p. 1225 b, 32 ff.; Xenophon,
Cyrop VIII, 2, 14—a comparison of the king with the shepherd.
For further examples of the stoics' and cynics' consequent pictures
of the king, see Lohmeyer, op. cit. pp. 48 f., notes 28-9.

[3] For its use as a style and divine predicate of hellenistic kings at
the end of the B.C. era, see Deissmann, *Licht vom Osten* (1923),
pp. 310 f.

Besides the use of *basileūs* for earthly or divine kings, the term is used for the ancient gods, especially frequently of Zeus as the *theōn basileūs* or just *basileūs* (Hesiod, *Theogony* 886, *Opera et dies* 668: here it is an epithet, or sometimes a cultic appellation (I.G. VII, 3073, 90; Ditt. Syll.[3] 1014, 110—Erythrae). For further *basileūs*-divinities (e.g. Hades in Aeschylus *Persae*, 627; I.G. I, 872; Poseidon, Apollo, Dionysus, Heracles) see Pauly-W. op cit. 82.

II. MELEK [1] AND MALKÛTH IN THE O.T.

1. KINGSHIP OF PEOPLE AND CITY

Kingship came to Israel in the great emergency caused by the attacks of the Philistines. Saul, who was at first, like his predecessors, a charismatic leader, was elected King over Israel. After his death, his mercenary general David was at first King of Judah until invested with the royal honours of Israel, which bound itself together with Judah in the form of allegiance to a common person. From the throne of his newly-won city-kingship over Jerusalem David ruled over the two kingdoms and protected the complicated constitution from disintegration, as a result of the transition from the traditional Israelite designation of the Leader by Yahweh to the ties of a dynasty. He saw the perpetually valid legitimisation of the Davidic house in the Davidic Covenant which Yahweh had made with him and his successors.[2] After the dissolution of the personal union at the death of Solomon, the Northern Kingdom knew only passing dynasties: the designation of the King by Yahweh became predominant. In Judah the house of David survived for four centuries on the throne, and in theory his lineage was traced to much later times still.

The relationship of the monarchy to the religious thought of Israel is conditioned by the circumstance that the monarchy emerged at a time when Israel's faith had developed in a highly unique fashion. In contrast to most of the old oriental peoples it did not

[1] *Melek* is common to all the semitic languages ; the verb *mâlak* must be denominative. The original meaning of the root is doubtful—possessor or arbiter. It is used but seldom in the O.T. in a purely metaphorical sense (Job xviii. 14).

[2] 2 Sam. vii and xxiii. 1-7.

grow up as an institution alongside religion and so become a fundamental element in religion, but was secondary, and came into a relationship with the already firmly established religious inheritance. Yahwism confronted it with a firmly founded criticism and very definite claims, but it received it tension-wise into its religion and especially into its hopes for the future.

In the early oriental courts, in whose centre stood a divine-human personality, the preconditions for the development of a court-style were conspicuously present, that is of a traditional ceremonial mode of addressing the king, greeting him as he ascends the throne, paying him homage with high-flown prayers and psalms, etc. In this sphere a quite definite repertory of stereotyped titles, similes, epithets and formularies had developed, and today we see clearly how strongly Israel had also participated in these common oriental forms.[1] When in the so-called Royal Psalms (Ps. ii. xx, xxi, xlv, lxxii, ci, cx, cxxxii) the King is promised divine sonship, the inheritance of the ends of the earth, when he is hailed as the King in whose reign a new era of peace and justice is dawning, here Israel has taken over many thoughts and formulations and incorporated them into her Yahwistic ideology. The King, in ancient eyes the very incorporation of the people, must of course, in Israel be pre-eminently the object of the gracious promises of Yahweh. But it is important to notice that the Israelite religion was stronger than the originally adopted forms: the King remains human: the O.T. knows nothing of any deification of the King, such as was the kernel of the court-styles of Babylon and Egypt.[2]

[1] Perhaps via old traditions of formerly Canaanite Jerusalem. Cf. Ps. cx.

[2] The only vestige that has escaped the severe censorship is Ps. xlv. 7. The declarations of divine sonship are formulas of adoption.

2. The Redeemer King

But now we must make a sharp distinction between the most extravagant utterances of the Israelite court-style and the belief in the Messiah. None of the Royal Psalms is messianic, for the ruler is everywhere thought of as present, it is present enemies who are addressed, etc.; there is nothing to indicate the eschatological expectation of a Redeemer King. And yet the court-style—so much we can now see—is the bridge to the messianic faith. The whole complex of religious-political concepts bound up with the actual king, what was expected of him, how he was addressed, the miracles attributed to him, all that became to a high degree the nursery of the messianic hope. This connection is not surprising, for the expected king is also a son of David. But problems still arise over the eschatological element infiltrating into the simple court-style. Why it was in Israel that that mystery-fraught projection into the *eschaton* appeared, for that we still have no satisfying explanations.[1] We need to remember that Babylon and Egypt, classical countries for the court-style, know no eschatology and no expectations of a Redeemer King at the end of time.

Although the belief in a Messiah feeds upon the ideology of the court-style for its form, its content links on to, and derives from, the person of David and especially the Davidic Covenant (2 Sam. vii). It is not David who will build a house for Yahweh—Yahweh will build David a house, and the latter's kingship is to last for ever. Here was a great promise whose complete, Yahweh-worthy, realisation (so it was increasingly realised) was still outstanding. It could not

[1] The unique Israelite conception of God, the belief in a powerful and dependable God, who is in a position to help Israel, is the root foundation of the religious hopes.

fall to the ground; if the present situation did not correspond, then it was carried forward into the future. Thus the hope of salvation in the re-establishment of the " fallen huts of David " in Amos (ix. 11) is implicitly based on the not yet fulfilled prophecy of Nathan (2 Sam. vii).

Now although the *terminus a quo* for the awakening of the messianic faith is David, that hope yet contains elements whose germs are not in the actual kingship. As early as the obscure prophecy in Gen. xlix. 8 ff. there are motifs of paradise involved (cf. Amos ix. 11-15). It is in no sense to be understood as a miserable formula of accommodation, for these tones are at their strongest in Isaiah, the messianic prophet *par excellence*. The shoot out of the stump of Jesse in Isa. ix and xi ushers in a new age of justice and of the peace of paradise. It is preceded by the annihilation of enemies, its essence consists of supernatural gifts. A similar expectation of a saving son of David is in Micah (v. 1 ff.). Rather less vigorous, yet clearly sketched, is Jeremiah's hope in the shoot (xxiii. 5 f.) and Ezekiel's expectation of the cedar-sprig (xvii. 22 ff., xxxiv. 23 ff., xxxvii. 24 f.). Deutero-Isaiah (xlv. 1 ff.) considered the Persian Cyrus, Zech. (vi. 9 ff.) the Davidic Zerubbabel, to be the King of the last age. This later projection of the messianic hope upon already existing historical characters represents an important change in eschatological conceptions. With the failure of this hope, specifically messianic prophecies become infrequent, and are almost entirely absent from the post-canonical literature,[1] until they come to life again immediately before the N.T. era.

---

[1] The Messianic hope seems to have been remarkably lively in the levitical circles which gave birth to Chronicles: cf. G. von Rad, *Geschichtsbild des Chronistischen Werkes* (1930), pp. 119 ff. Zechariah ix. 9 is hardly datable. In Dan. vii. 13, there was probably mention of a Messiah in the mythological material, but the editor

If one disregards the enthusiastic phraseology of the court-style and the already mentioned specifically Israelite element of the eschatological, both of which are part and parcel of the Hebrew messianic hope, one comes upon a very considerable remnant of mythological conceptions, which are certainly not an original contribution of the prophets, but which are far from easy to derive from ancient Hebrew religion. In particular, the indications of a pretemporal existence of this Saviour-King [1] and the indissoluble link of this personality with an age of paradisal fruitfulness lead to the conjecture that certain non-Israelite mythical elements [2] of a returning primeval King or of some paradisal *Urmensch* have become fused with the firm promises of the Davidic Covenant. Although the expectations linked with the Messiah take many forms, yet all the evidence points to the fact that the Messiah appears as a Prince of Peace for his own people, so much so that his advent is remarkably unconnected with the wars and capturings of enemies that precede his era. The transition to the new age is not fought for by him,[3] but he stands over beyond this last battle as the ruler in a paradisal era. Another peculiarity of most of the texts about the coming of the Messiah is the shunning of the title *melek*: " in it lurks something impious, all too human, violence and pressure ".[4]

has changed his material. There is no Messiah mentioned in the Servant-songs of Deutero-Isaiah, cf. *Z.A.W.* 47 (1925), pp. 90 ff.; 48 (1926), pp. 242 ff.; 50 (1928), pp. 156 ff.; 51 (1929), pp. 255 ff. Incidentally, the O.T. does not know of *mâshîach* as a title for the eschatological King.

[1] Esp. Mic. v. 1; cf. Sellin, *Prophetismus*, pp. 178 f.

[2] R. Kittel (op. cit. pp. 64 ff.) looks for the origins of the isaianic picture of the Messiah in the Egyptian myth of Osiris.

[3] Isa. xi. 4 is hardly an exception: without touching a weapon, and with the breath of his lips he combats his adversaries miraculously.

[4] W. Caspari, *Echtheit, Hauptbegriff und Gedankengang der messianischen Weissagung Jesaiah* ix (1908), p. 14.

Opposition to the empirical monarchy seems to be a feature of most of the messianic prophecies.

3. YAHWEH AS KING

It is clear, however, that the hope of a Messiah is by no means paramount in the O.T., but occurs relatively seldom in it. There is much more evidence for the belief in another supernatural kingship which directs the present and future—the sovereignty of Yahweh. The relationship of these conceptions to a messianic kingdom cannot be reduced to a simple formula.[1] It is not possible to draw out two independent traditions, for Isaiah, the most powerful of the messianic prophets, speaks of Yahweh as King, and so do Micah and Jeremiah; on the other hand the Psalms, which know nothing of the eschatological king, provide the most copious and the weightiest evidence for the kingship of Yahweh.[2]

The use of the term *melek* of the godhead is a characteristic of the ancient East (cf. among Israel's neighbours, Melkart, Milcom, Chemoshmelek)—indeed this divine epithet is probably of semitic origin. It provides the best description of the relationship between God and man: God is Lord, He demands obedience, but in return gives His people protection and help. In Israel the emergence of this designation can be traced fairly precisely. The references are to be found, as one might expect, after the advent of the empirical

---

[1] Unfortunately this problem has hardly been touched upon in the recent lively discussion over O.T. eschatology. Caspari, op. cit. pp. 12 ff., shows convincingly that the messianic figure of Isa. ix is no independent ruler. The terms *sar* and *yôçêr* indicate that he is responsible to power above. In Jer. (e.g. xxiii. 5) and Ezek. (xxxvii. 24) the Messiah is *melek*.

[2] A special attitude is shown in this as in other respects by the deuteronomic theology: it knows neither the conception of Yahweh's kingship nor a messianic hope.

Kingship: Num. xxiii. 21; Deut. xxxiii. 5; 1 Kings xxii. 19; Isa. vi. 5, must be the earliest examples.

The conception of Yahweh's Kingship has, however, very various shades of meaning in the O.T. There are passages which stress the timelessness of Yahweh's sovereignty, which comprehends past and future alike (Exod. xv. 18; 1 Sam. xii. 12; Ps. cxlv. 11 ff., cxlvi. 10), others accentuate the element of expectation (Isa. xxiv. 23, xxxiii. 22; Zeph. iii. 15; Obad. 21; Zech. xiv. 16 f.). The present is not enough to do justice to these claims, the concept of Yahweh's kingship gets drawn into the stream of eschatology, towards which it had always shown a propensity[1]: it is hoped that Yahweh will show Himself as King hereafter. But even the most pointedly eschatological passages do not for one moment suggest that Yahweh's kingship is not already a present reality. It is only the final manifestation of the complete sovereignty that is awaited. A third group of prophecies is to be found in Ps. xlvii, xciii, xcvi, xcvii, xcix (the number could probably be increased) and their peculiarity is pin-pointed in the verb *mâlak* (used of Yahweh—" Yahweh has become King "). These are the Coronation Psalms, which are obviously the high point of a festival which celebrated ceremonially (and dramatically?) Yahweh's ascent of His throne.[2] These Psalms proclaim no eschatological event, but a present actually experienced in the liturgy.

A really concrete picture of Yahweh's sovereignty is to be found only in the last-named group, and the officials of this ceremonial may in fact have considered the expectation of an eschatological king as a contradiction of their faith. On the other hand, the other

[1] O. Eissfeldt, *Jahwe als König*, *Z.A.W.* 50 (1928), pp. 81 ff.

[2] Cf. Mowinckel, *Psalmenstudien* II. But he greatly exaggerates the significance of this festival, and the ingenious derivation of Israelite eschatology from it has since been invalidated by his later dating of it. (*Z.A.W.* 52 (1930), p. 267, note 3.)

passages belong far more to the traditional poetical
style which could on occasion combine without great
tension with the belief in a coming Messiah.   That the
two conceptions, which originally no doubt grew up
quite independently, were later able to come together
in harmonious fusion can be seen in Chronicles, which
strongly picks up Yahweh's not yet fulfilled promise to
David: David's descendant rules in Yahweh's *malkûth*:
that is the sense of the Davidic Covenant, as understood
by the later Chronicler (1 Chron. xvii. 14, xxviii. 5,
xxix. 23; 2 Chron. ix. 8, xiii. 8).

The exact nature of Yahweh's Kingdom, however,
is not discernible from the majority of the passages.
The many predications in the hymns are mostly silent
as to whether Yahweh is understood to be King of
Israel or King of the world.[1]   Nevertheless the pre-
exilic passages mostly describe Yahweh as Israel's King
and promise help, deliverance, justice and joy for the
chosen people,[2] whereas in the exilic and post-exilic
eras there are also pointers to Yahweh's kingship over
the world.[3]   Thus the designation of Yahweh as king
certainly seems to make expressly clear and concrete
his power, majesty and helpfulness, but these conceptions were so common and so little bound up with the
specific concept of king that there was no hesitation in
combining it with quite other thought-forms.   Micah
mingles it with the figure of the shepherd (v. 3) and
Deutero-Isaiah speaks in parallelism of creator, redeemer and King (xliii. 14 f.).   The essence of God's
malkûth is seldom more precisely sketched.   But the
reason why that can be stated is that it is always

---

[1] Jer. xlvi. 18, xlviii. 15, li, 57; Ps. v. 3, xxiv. 7 ff.; Dan. iv. 34.
[2] Num. xxiii. 21; Jer. viii. 1; Zeph. iii. 15;   Mic. x. 12 f.,
iv. 6 ff.; but also Isa. xli. 21, xliii. 15, xliv. 6.
[3] Jer. x. 7, 10 ff. (Jer. x. 1-16 is hardly jeremianic); Zech.
xiv. 9, 16 f.; Mal. i. 14; Ps. xxii. 29, xlvii. 3, 8.

described as immanent. Even in such late passages as Isa. xxiv. 23 and Zech. xiv. 9, 16, Yahweh is to reign over the whole earth, have His throne in Jerusalem and be worshipped there by all peoples (cf. Obad. 21).[1]

4. MALKÛTH

The noun *malkûth* is one of the few older Hebrew abstract terms, from which the large number of later conceptions derived. Its initial meaning is kingship; its use in the sense of royal sovereignty, in relation to the concrete sphere of power, is a simple inflection from the root meaning.[2]

[1] This problem is dealt with by Martin Buber in his large-scale work on the Kingdom of God—*das Königtum Gottes* (1932). His thesis, however, is original in so far as the O.T. evidence for Yahweh as King has not received the interpretation among theologians in general which Buber assumes. Even if one declines to follow Eissfeldt (op. cit. p. 104) in regarding Isa. vi. 5 as the first instance, on the ground that he is being too lexicographical, it remains true that Yahweh is in no case described as King before the era of the monarchy. In any case there is no exegetical basis in the texts for interpreting the Sinai covenant monarchically. In general the predication of Yahweh as King belongs far more to the poetical exaggerations of an exalted style rather than to any specially significant evidence for a basic belief. Buber sharply contrasts the *malk*, the " Führer-god " with the Baal. Had he said " Yahweh " instead of " *malk* ", one would agree; but when, it may be asked, in the bitter struggle versus Baal-worship—e.g. in Hosea or Deuteronomy—is Yahweh referred to as " *malk* "? Buber cites many passages which, in one way or another, declare that Yahweh has " led " Israel: yet the theological term " *malk* ", in the sense maintained, is not mentioned. Rather is the specific importance of those other passages where it does really belong (i.e. in the ceremonial or eschatological sense) thereby diminished.

[2] *Mamlākah* differs little from *malkûth*; similarly *melûkah* also means sovereignty. The latter term is used only in a *religious* sense in Ps. xxii. 29 and Obad. 21 of Yahweh's kingly power in the present and at the end of time.

The term *malkûth* is nearly always used in the O.T. in a secular sense, meaning political kingship (1 Sam. xx. 31; 1 Kings ii. 12). Religious thought before Daniel made little use of this term. However, in keeping with the naming of Yahweh as a *melek*, God's sphere of sovereignty is occasionally described as His *malkûth*.[1] A slight anticipation of the frequent eschatological use of it in the post-canonical writings is to be found in the slight corrections of the inherited text in the work of the Chronicler. In 2 Sam. vii. 16, David was confirmed in his *mamlâkah*, which word was understood in a much more secular sense than in 1 Chron. xvii. 14, where David appears as set over Yahweh's *malkûth*. In 1 Chron. xxviii. 5, Solomon sits upon the throne of the *malkûth* of Yahweh. This manner of speaking is not to be understood eschatologically. The Davidic Kingdom is here understood as Yahweh's *malkûth:* on the " throne of Yahweh " (1 Chron. xxix. 23; 2 Chron. ix. 8) sit the descendants of David. But these nuances are significant, for the Chronicler, living in an age when the Davidic monarchy could be but a distant memory, betrays an interest in the realisation of Yahweh's *malkûth*, which although not eschatological, was none the less actual and real.

The sharp apocalyptic distinction between the present and future ages, first found in Daniel, brings with it a much more incisive definition of the term " Kingdom of God ". Although in Dan. vii each of the transcendent-born kingdoms is described as *malkû*, this term, when used of the last, the " Kingdom of the Saints " has its special colouring. God can pass on the *malkû* to whomsoever He will (Dan. ii. 44, iv. 22); He gives it to His people and thereby establishes an eternal

[1] Ps. ciii. 19, cxlv. 11, 13; Dan. iii. 33. Cf. *melûkah* in Ps. xxii. 29.

Kingdom (Dan. vii. 27). But this passage does not speak of God's *malkûth*, and Yahweh is not King: it is a question of a succession of human kingdoms until the *malkû* of the saints comes as the last—so is the coming " Son of Man " interpreted (Dan. vii. 16 ff.). This strongly nationalist hope for the *malkû* occurs very frequently in subsequent apocalyptic [1] literature (1 Enoch lxxxiv. 2, xc. 30, xcii. 4: *Assumption of Moses,* x. 1 ff., and *passim*).[2]

[1] For the use of *malkûth* in rabbinic Judaism, see pp. 16 ff.
[2] Cf. Bousset-Gressmann, op. cit. pp. 214 ff.

III. MALKÛTH SHÂMAYIM IN RABBINIC LITERATURE [1]

1. *Its Origin*

THE late Jewish conception of *malkûth shâmayim* [Kingdom of the Heavens] owes it genesis to the general tendency in late Judaism to avoid verbal references to God, such as are used in the O.T., and to replace them by abstract formulations. It is, therefore, closely connected with the term *shekînah*. Just as the latter is simply a substitute for the O.T. sentence *shâkhan Yahweh* "God dwells" . . . "God is present", [2] so the expression *malkûth shâmayim* appears in late Judaism in place of the O.T. "*malk Yahweh*", "God is King", cf. supra, pp. 9 ff. [3]

Thus the Targums frequently replace the O.T. term by *malkûtha' de Y.*—"the Kingdom of God"; for example the *Onkelos Targum* to Exod. xv. 18 has *Y malkûtheh qâ'êm*, "God's Kingdom stands firm" for the O.T. *Yahweh yimlôk*—"Yahweh reigns"; that to Isa. xxiv. 23 has "God's Kingdom is revealed" for the O.T. "The Lord is King". So also in Isa. xxxi. 4, xl. 9, lii. 7; Mic. iv. 7; Zech. xiv. 9. [4] On the other hand the Targum keeps the actual O.T. expression in

[1] *Melek* in the rabbinic literature calls for no special treatment, as here (unlike the O.T.) all the significance of the word-group is to be found in *malkûth*: hence everything of importance about the former in late Judaism (God as King, the Messiah-King) is included in this section, in so far as it has not already been said in the O.T. section.

[2] Cf. S-B, ii. p. 314. *Sifre*, Num. i or v. 3, etc.

[3] A third similar late Jewish abstract formation is the Targum term *mêmra' de Y.* (rearrangement of the sentence "*'âmar Yahweh*") and no more—no "hypostasis". Cf. S-B, ii, pp. 302 ff.

[4] Cf. Dalman, *Worte Jesu*, i, pp. 79 and 83.

Ezek. xx. 33; Ps. xlvii. 9, xciii. 1, xcvi. 10, xcvii. 1, xcix. 1, cxlvi. 10.

Since in late Judaism the name *Yahweh* was replaced by *'ᵃdônây* in liturgical use (scripture reading in the synagogue), the Targums quite logically write *malkûth' dᵉY*, which was read as *m da '*ᵃ*donây*. In ordinary conversation, however, the name of God was avoided by means of replacing it by *shâmayim*, " Heaven ". Hence in the rabbinic literature, apart from the Targums, one always finds the expression *malkûth shâmayim*, of which the slavishly literal translation into Greek is βασιλεία τῶν οὐρανῶν (Matt.) but the actually correct rendering is βασιλεία τοῦ θεοῦ (Mark, Luke). In the rabbinic vocabulary even *shâmayim* was later—probably round about A.D. 100—itself replaced as a name for God by *hammâqôm*, " the place ". Only in some stereotyped expressions [1] does *shâmayim* survive as a name for God, as also in *malkûth shâmayim*.

From this origin of the expression it is at once clear that *malkûth shâmayim* can never mean " the Kingdom of God " in the sense of the territory ruled over by Him. The expression describes simply the fact that God is King, thus meaning always the " being King ", " Kingship " on the part of God.[2]

Malkûth shâmayim is therefore from the very start a purely theological conception formed in late Judaism, not a transference of the secular term *malkûth* to the

---

[1] Listed in S-B, i, p. 172, under A; and i, pp. 862 ff.

[2] Cf. Dalman, *Worte Jesu*, i, p. 77 (" King's *régime*, not king's realm "). But he establishes the point merely empirically: " An oriental *Reich* is no State in our sense, no ' constituted ' people or land, but a rule which embraces a definite area." Actually the point lies in the meaning of the term itself. To turn the conception into a " more or less " as in RGG (2), iv. 181 (Mundle), " denotes *less* the geographical conception of an empire *than* the fact of the royal power of a king " is incomprehensible.

religious sphere.[1] In the rabbinic literature *malkûth*
by itself always means the secular government, the
Roman Empire,[2] by which is meant not so much the
State as such as the Roman suzerainty as seen from the
point of view of a subject of this State, " the authority
which exercises power over him ".[3] With this secular
malkûth the *malkûth shâmayim*, which developed later out
of quite different roots, long after the term had been
coined, is, on occasion, contrasted.[4] The unique,
original meaning of *malkûth shâmayim* (namely the
abstract counterpart of the clause " God is King ")
was, nevertheless, always clearly understood by the
Rabbis. This is shown by the fact that in the rabbinic
literature those Bible passages in which God is called
" King " are described as *malkîyôth* i.e. " *malkûth*-
verses ", " Kingship-verses ".[5]

2. *Its Use*

The detailed development of the conception calls for
no comprehensive survey, as all the rabbinical material
about *malkûth shâmayim* has often been collected. Here
we must above all set out the essential insights for the
understanding of the coverage of the term. The first
point to notice is that the expression is rare in the
rabbinic literature and not nearly as important as, e.g.
in the preaching of Jesus. The phrase occurs chiefly

[1] The transference actually took place much earlier—in the
time of David—with *melek*. (Cf. supra, p. 9, ad fin.)

[2] S-B, i, p. 183, gives many instances.

[3] In the case of this *malkûth*, the " more or less " of note 2 above
is in place.

[4] Only in three passages, which (according to the authors named)
date from the third century A.D. is the *malkûth shâmayim* contrasted
with the *malkûth hâ'âreç*—Genesis *rabba* ix (7b), *Pesikta* 51 a (and
parallels): Babylon *berakoth* 58 a (S-B, i, pp. 175 f. under h).

[5] Cf. *Rosh Hashana*, iv. 5; *Sifre*, Num. 77, on x. 10. See on
this Moore, ii, pp. 210, 373.

only in two modes of speech which both cover its theologically important range. One is *qibbêl ʿôl malkûth shâmayim*—" to take the yoke of God's sovereignty upon oneself ",[1] i.e. (exactly corresponding to the definition of the phrase given above) " to recognise God as King and Lord over oneself ", " to recognise one God as King and reject all other gods ". The expression thus indicates acceptance of Jewish monotheism, as every believing Jew daily expresses it in the *sheˡmaʿ* (Deut. vi. 4: " Hear, O Israel, the Lord our God is One "). So *qibbêl ʿôl malkûth shâmayim* often means simply " to recite the *sheˡmaʿ* ".[2]

Thus *malkûth shâmayim* here means something for or against which man must decide in a free choice. For there is always also the possibility open to him of rejecting God as King and Lord (" casting off the yoke of God's sovereignty "); and from this possibility it follows that God's sovereignty is not patently apparent —otherwise it would be a question merely of recognition, whether voluntary or not, on the part of all men that God is King. On the other hand there is only real decision (i.e. decision which everybody must make and which is at the same time binding and valid) when the possibility of decision is limited, or has an end. And here we come to the second mode of speech in which *malkûth shâmayim* commonly occurs. For this end, *qêç—τέλος*, which terminates the possibility of accepting or rejecting God's Kingship through a free act of will, is of course the manifestation of God's sovereignty. This manifestation is the oft repeated prayer of Judaism,[3] and in the same way the Targums speak frequently of the end of time when the sovereignty of God

[1] Cf. S-B, i, pp. 173 ff. *passim*.
[2] S-B, i, pp. 177 ff. under n.
[3] Cf. the two prayers out of Tractate *Soferim* in S-B, i, p. 179; other instances are also cited.

becomes manifest.[1] Thus *malkûth shâmayim* is obviously, in the theology of late Judaism, a purely eschatological phrase, in the strictest sense of that word.

3. *Its divorce from national hopes*

Now it is especially worthy of notice that from all this thought the " people of Israel " is completely absent. In this case nationality is in no sense an element of significance for the religious attitudes of man. Here man stands before God as an individual (who must make a decision) just as " man ", not as a citizen of some country. In this there has reached its terminus in the rabbinic theology a development of religious thought which had its starting point in the O.T. prophets. But the other channel of O.T. piety —religion determined by nationality—which is above all alive in Law and Liturgy, has certainly not vanished in the rabbinic theology. On the contrary, the Rabbis always stressed the religious prerogative of the people of Israel, according to which nationality is determinative for man's position in the sight of God.[2] This thought has also a certain part to play in the conception *malkûth shâmayim*. Often in Jewish prayers, God is addressed as King of Israel.[3] The same thought occurs when it is stated that the patriarch Abraham made God King upon earth [4] in that he was the first to recognise the One God as King and Lord, or when it is said that Israel—the people as such—on

---

[1] Cf. the passages cited above p. 15; also Moore, op. cit. ii, p. 374, n. 3. *Sibylline Oracles* iii. 47 f. (φανεῖται) and Luke xix. 19 (μέλλει ἡ βασιλεία τοῦ θεοῦ ἀναφαίνεσθαι).

[2] Tractate *Sanhedrin* x. 1. All Israel shares in the world to come.

[3] S-B, i, p. 175 under e. Cf. *Psalms of Solomon* v. 18 f. and xvii. 3. The connection with the ceremonial piety of the Royal Psalms is clear.

[4] Cf. *Sifre*, Deut. 313, on xxxii. 10 (S-B, i. p. 173 under c).

the Red Sea or on Mount Sinai, through the confession
of the true God and through the acceptance of His
Torah " took upon itself the yoke of God's sovereignty ".[1]

Both these channels—religion determined by nationality and the religion of the individual—run side by
side and independently in all late Judaism. This
antinomy arose from the fact that each channel of
statements, present in various O.T. writings, as a result
of the canonicity of the O.T. for later Judaism, was
the word of God, and equally so. But the remarkable
thing is that there is not ever any indication sanctioned
in the Holy Scripture to correlate the two channels side
by side into one complete theological system. Such a
tendency is completely absent : the rabbinic writers
did not feel this antinomy as a tension or embarrass-
ment.

Thus, in considering *malkûth shâmayim*, the position
is that the occasional connexion with popular thought
noticed is merely a traditional link with the relative
O.T. quotations,[2] whereas the liveliness and significance
of the idea in late Judaism depends upon the strongly
religious sequence of thought first developed above.
Thus *malkûth shâmayim* is one of the few, if not the only,
quite strong and pure conceptions in late Judaism :
the ἔσχατον of the " manifestation of the *malkûth
shâmayim* " as that which demands the decision of each
individual to " take upon himself " or " reject " " the
yoke of the *malkûth shâmayim* ".

4. *Its relationship to the Messiah*

Thus we reach the clear definition of the conception
vis-à-vis the expectation of a Messiah-King at the end
of time. Whereas *malkûth shâmayim* as a phrase is

[1] S-B, i, p. 172, d and p. 174; *Sifre*, Lev. xviii. 6.
[2] Cf. p. 19, note 3.

purely eschatological and has not arisen in the course
of an historical development, so the expectation of a
Messiah-King developed gradually out of the at first
purely secular expectation of an Israelite King, who
would restore the Kingdom of Israel in the whole
extent and the glory of the ideal Davidic Kingdom,
into an eschatological hope—but not strictly eschatological. The " coming of the Messiah " is placed
rather *before* the ἔσχατον in Jewish thought.[1] The
difference may be reduced to this : the concept of a
Messiah in late Judaism was always an expression of a
hope for the end of time which knew God in the first
instance as the King of Israel and therefore regarded
as the goal of God's plan of salvation the eventual
inauguration of the Kingdom of the people of Israel
with the Messiah as King, of a King to whom all other
peoples are subject ; in *malkûth shâmayim*, on the other
hand, the purely religious concept of the ἔσχατον is
expressed in all its exaltation (" God all in all "),
wherein there is no longer any place for the special
national idea of the link with Israel.

Thus the two conceptions are quite heterogeneous.
True, they appear not seldom side by side as the two
points towards which the hope of the pious Jew, the
national and the purely religious hope, is directed.[2]
But nowhere are they closely related. Nowhere do we
find the thought that the Kingdom of the Messiah is
the *malkûth shâmayim* or that the Messiah inaugurates it
through his actions, or vice versa. Such a connexion
with the conception of a Messiah is impossible if one
starts with the definite concept of the *malkûth shâmayim*.

[1] Cf. S-B, iv, pp. 968 f.
[2] E.g. at the beginning of the Kaddish prayer: " May he set
up his royal sovereignty . . . and bring with it his Messiah."
For the whole train of thought see above all Moore, ii, pp. 371-5.

IV. BASILEIA (*TOU THEOU*) IN
HELLENISTIC JUDAISM

In essentials the LXX agrees with the Hebrew, or Aramaic (Daniel), originals in the few passages where God's Kingdom is mentioned. But in the LXX there are also a few passages which are specifically Greek or hellenistic, and have no Hebrew original in the canonical O.T.—e.g. Wisd. vi. 20 : *epithumia sophiās anagei epi basileian*. This passage summarises the high value and the accessibility of Wisdom : to aspire after her leads to leadership. True, in this sixth chapter of Wisdom there are also references to the *basileia tou theou* : in vi. 4 the Kings of the earth are addressed as the *hupēretai tēs autou* (i.e. God's) *basileiās;* in x. 10 it is said of Wisdom that she showed the righteous man " God's Kingdom ". But the use of *basileia* by itself (vi. 20; cf. x. 14) points to the sovereignty of the wise. This connects with 4 Macc. ii. 23—God has given man a law, by following which he βασιλεύσει βασιλείαν σώφρονά τε καὶ δικαίον καὶ ἀγαθὴν καὶ ἀνδρείαν: the *basileia* is identified with the four main virtues.

Yet more clearly and comprehensively is this popular-philosophical ethicalisation of the concept of *basileia* carried to its furthest lengths in Philo. So far as the general use of the term is concerned, there is no question but that the predominant meaning here is monarchy, royal sovereignty, and leadership in general. The actor puts on the *parasēma* (token) *tēs basileias*. This meaning also occurs in the plural; beside those invested with royal dignity stand those invested with generalship—οἱ τῆς βασιλείας καὶ ἡγεμονίας ἀναψάμενοι, *De Plantatione*, 67. Nimrod had Babylon as the ἀρχὴ τῆς βασιλείας, *De Gigantibus*, 66. On various occasions

Philo gives a definition of the term: *basileia* is linked
in hendiadys with *archē* (*De Mutatione Nominum*, 15, *De
Vita Mosis* I, 148, *Quod omnis probus liber sit*, 117); it
stands next to *politeia* (*De Plantatione*, 56); it is more
than *ochlokratia*, *De Fuga et Inventione*, 10; the earthly
basileia has two tasks, ποιμενικὴ μελέτη καὶ προγυμνασία
(*De Vita Mosis* I, 60). Furthermore, *basileia* is re-
peatedly linked, even identified, with *archē*. The
basileia of Moses, meaning his leadership, is parallel
with his *nomothesia*, *prophēteia* and *archierōsunē* (*De
Praemiis et Poenis*, 53), with his *nomothetikē hexis*, *hierōsunē*
and *prophēteia* (*De Vita Mosis* II, 187). The same is
found if one looks back to the first book of the *Vita* of
Moses, which shows that the whole of this first book
treats of the *basileia* of Moses (i. 333 f.; cf. ii. 66). In
a special discussion the difference between *basileia*
(secular Kingship) and *archierōsunē* (high-priesthood) is
clarified in such a way as to give precedence to the
latter over the former, because the latter is as good as
theou therapeia, and *basileia* as good as *epimeleia anthrōpōn*,
so that both terms are distinguished according to their
objects (*theos* or *anthrōpoi*)—*Legatio ad Gaium*, 278; cf.
De Virtutibus, 54. *Hierōsunē* is worthy of an *eusebēs anēr*,
and to be preferred to freedom, even to *basileia* (*De
specialibus Legibus* i. 57). In a definition of *basileia*, of
which the *dogmata* and *nomoi* are to be observed, we
find: "*basileian. . . . sophian einai legomen, epei kai ton
sophon basilea* (*De Migratione Abrahami*, 147). Similar
is the inflexion *hē tou sophou basileia* (*De Abrahamo*, 261;
cf. *De Somniis* ii. 243 f.). Correspondingly Saul is to
learn from Samuel *ta tēs basileias dikaia* (*De Migratione
Abrahami*, 196). That the first man gives their names
to the animals is understood to be *sophias kai basileias to
ergon* (connexion of wisdom and power) (*De Opificio
Mundi*, 148). Meanwhile the precise meaning of *basileia*
is defined as being merely royal sovereignty as seen in

the rule of the wise as the true king (*De Sacrificiis Abelis et Caeni*, 49). In respect of the wise King Abraham *aretē* (virtue) is defined as *archē* and *basileia* (*De Somniis* ii. 244). Similar language is used of *nous:* the operators of *nous* bring it to *tēn hēgemoniān kai basileiān tōn anthrōpeiōn pragmatōn* (*De Specialibus Legibus* i. 334). The opposite of all this is τὸ ἡδέως ζῆν, to regard which as *hegemonia* and *basileia* is a delusion (*De Ebrietate*, 216).

Does Philo speak in these passages of God's sovereignty, or at least also of God's sovereignty? Does he speak of God's sovereignty at all? Yes and no! *Tou theou* appears attributively once, in that the rule of a King is compared with the *basileia tou theou* (*De Specialibus Legibus* iv. 164), and also once predicatively —ἡ βασιλεία τίνος; ἆρ' οὐχὶ μόνου θεοῦ; (*De Mutatione Nominum*, 135). God's sovereignty may be in mind when the building of the tower of Babel is regarded as the *kathairesis tēs aiōniou basileias* (*De Somniis* ii. 285). God is clothed with *anantagōnistos* (invincible) *kai anaphairetos* (completely secure) *basileia* (*De Specialibus Legibus* i. 207). Abraham as true king, i.e. King of wisdom, comes from God, since God *tēn tou sophou basileian oregei* (*De Abr.* 261). Moses shows himself to be a being superior to the first cause who guides the world, χρώμενον αὐτεξουσίῳ καὶ αὐτοκράτορι βασιλείᾳ (*Quis Rerum divinarum Heres sit*, 301).

To a future *basileia* Philo gives only one hint when he once cites Num. xxiv. 7 (Balaam's messianic prophecy) in connexion with the LXX: ἡ τοῦδε βασιλεία καθ' ἑκάστην ἡμέραν πρὸς ὕψος ἀρθήσεται (*De Vita Mosis* I, 290). Here too the Kingship is conceived ethically.[1]

[1 Philo also portrays the *substance* of a future 'messianic' kingdom which will come 'when men turn to God' in *De Praemiis et Poenis*, 85–126, also citing Num. xxiv. 7.]

Our summary of all the *basileia*-passages [1] in Philo makes it certain that the royal sovereignty is never understood eschatologically. Far more is *basileia* a chapter in moral teaching.[2] The true king is the wise man. Thus Philo agrees with the paeans to the wise man usual in ancient philosophy. The wise man as the true *basileūs* [3] transcends ordinary earthly kings and is thereby to be honoured as divine. This conception determines also Philo's philosophico-religious language about the *basileia tou sophou*. This interpretation derives ultimately from ancient philosophy, but its form comes from the Greek Bible, which Philo interprets and reinterprets in the same manner as has happened in some of the above-mentioned LXX passages. To be sure, it must be mentioned that behind this ethicalisation and anthropologising lie certain tendencies found in late judaism in general. But in spite of a clearly visible influence of this kind, apocalyptic and rabbinic judaism held firm to the thought of God's sovereignty depending upon God's free decision.[4] But Philo has completely changed the original *basileia*-concept, although as exegete (in contrast to Josephus) he has no hesitation in speaking of the *basileia tou theou*.[5]

---

[1] Cf. H. Leisegang's *Indices*, reading v. 14, 21 for v. 142, 1 and deriving $\tau\tilde{\omega}\nu\ \beta\alpha\sigma\iota\lambda\epsilon\acute{\iota}\omega\nu$ not from $\acute{\eta}\ \beta\alpha\sigma\iota\lambda\epsilon\acute{\iota}\alpha$, but from $\tau\grave{\alpha}\ \beta\alpha\sigma\acute{\iota}\lambda\epsilon\iota\alpha$, in v. 230, 8.

[2] In the index to E. Brehier's *Les idées philosophiques et religieuses de Philon d'Alexandrie* (1908), there are many passages under " Vertu " but none under " royaume (de Dieu) "; cf. I. Heinemann, *Philons griechische and jüdische Bildung* (1932).

[3] Cf. supra, p. 1, ad fin.

[4] Cf. G. Gloege, *Reich Gottes und Kirche im Neuen Testament* (1929), 19 ff. In that section Philo is not valued more highly than is late Judaism.

[5] Cf. A. Schlatter, *Die Theologie des Judentums nach dem Bericht des Josephus* (1932), p. 49, note 1.

Josephus never uses the term *basileia tou theou*. Only in *Antiquities* vi. 60 is *basileia* mentioned in connexion with God. Whereas the Palestinian Judaism from which he sprang spoke of the *malkûth shâmayim* in the eschatological sense alongside its references to the present, Josephus used the word *theokratia* (*Contra Apionem* ii. 165) for the present situation of the congregation. Instead of *basileūs* and *basileia* he says *hēgemōn* and *hēgemonia*, in that he ascribes to the Roman emperor not *basileia* but *hēgemonia*.[1] This situation is probably to be explained (i) by the fact that Josephus may (as he did in general) have refrained from speaking of the eschatological-messianic outlook of his people which is bound up with *basileia*, and (ii) from the circumstance that he, as an historian living and writing in Rome, was indebted to Hellenism and at the same time was completely dependent upon his sources.[2]

[1] So A. Schlatter, *Wie sprach Josephus von Gott?* (1910), pp. 11 f.
[2] Cf. G. Hölscher in his article on Josephus in Pauly-W. ix. 1955: "In his portrayal of Jewish history Josephus entirely renounced any independent use of the text of the Bible, whether in its Greek or Hebrew version, and his material is almost completely, even down to nearly all points of detail, taken from written sources."

V. *BASILEUS* AND ITS CORRELATES IN THE N.T.

A. BASILEUS

THIS word, meaning king, is used in the N.T. of men and God(s), and also of intermediate beings. Of theological importance is the fact that in the N.T., closely connected and in agreement with the O.T. and Jewish usage, both God and Christ (the Messiah Jesus) receive this title, and human kings receive a diminishing assessment of honour.

1. (*a*) *Earthly Kings* in general (unnamed) and special cases (named) in the N.T. are regarded explicitly and implicitly as contrasted with, or at least inferior to, God as King, or the Messiah-King. Those named king (as in the non-biblical literature) are Pharaoh (Acts vii. 10—then replaced by " another king ", Acts vii. 18; also Heb. xi. 23, 27); Herod the Great (Matt. ii. 1, 3, 9; Luke i. 5); also Herod Antipas—never strictly king—(Matt. xiv. 9; Mark vi. 14, 22, 25, 26, 27); Herod Agrippa I (Acts xii. 1 and 20); Herod Agrippa II (Acts xxv. 13, 14, 24, 26; xxvi. 2, 7, 13, 19, 26, 27, 30); also the Nabataean Aretas (2 Cor. xi. 32); further (according to oriental custom) [1] the Roman Emperor (1 Tim. ii. 2; 1 Pet. ii. 13, 17; Rev. xvii. 9 f.; cf. 1 Clement xxxvii. 3). All such kings are kings of the earth, of the nations— *tēs gēs* (Matt. xvii. 25; Acts iv. 26; Rev. i. 5, vi. 15, xvii. 2, 18, xviii. 9, xix. 19, xxi. 24); *tōn ethnōn* (Luke xxii. 25); *tēs oikoumenēs holēs* (Rev. xvi. 14). The description and appraisal of the "Kings of the earth" have been taken from Ps. ii. 2, lxxxviii. 28 [2], etc. As in the O.T.,

---

[1] Cf. Deissmann, *Licht vom Osten*, pp. 310 f.
[[2] i.e. Ps. lxxxix. 28 in Hebrew and English.]

the earthly king is not given the rank of divine status
as in the old oriental court-style, since this status is
granted only to Yahweh or to his Messiah-King. In
the Apocalypse this contrast is further heightened, in
that in answer to the contemporary titles of the Roman
emperors and their oriental prototypes it is precisely
and only the One Almighty God who is designated
basileus tōn ethnōn (Rev. xv. 3) and the Messiah-King is
called the great King, the King of Kings and Lord of
Lords (Rev. xix. 16; cf. xvii. 14). Earthly kings with
their power are subjected by God and Christ to the
sons of the Kingdom of God, who are taken out of the
realms of earthly royal power, who serve one another
as brothers (Matt. xvii. 25 f.; Luke xxii. 25). Before
hēgemones and *basileis* will Christians for Christ's sake be
led for judgement at the approach of God's Kingdom
(Matt. x.18; Mark xiii. 9; Luke xxi. 12). *En tois
oikois tōn basileōn* (v.l. *basileiōn*) are to be found the
people clad in soft raiment, but no prophet like John
the Baptist (Matt. xi. 8). From earthly kings and even
prophets remain hidden the things which are clear to
the children of the Kingdom (Luke x. 24). Kings
occupied with war (Luke xiv. 31) are, like the Gentiles
and Jews, to hear the good news of God's Kingdom
(Acts ix. 15; cf. Rev. x. 11). At the end of days the
kings of the East are the rod of God's chastisement and
are then themselves annihilated (Rev. xvi. 12, cf. xvi.
14, xvii. 2, 9, 12, 18, xviii. 3, 9, xix. 18 f.). On the
other hand, the possibility also exists that they will
subject themselves in obedience (Rev. xxi. 24).

(*b*) No more and no less than an earthly king is also
an intermediate being like *Abbadon*, Lord of the Spirits
of the underworld (Rev. ix. 11).

(*c*) A special case is presented by the royalty of
earthly men like David and Melchizedek. No matter
how the monarchy appeared and maintained itself in

the Hebrew era (cf. Acts xiii. 21—the Israelites asked God for a King and received Saul), in the N.T. eyes David, as ancestor of Jesus Christ is a King forechosen by God (Matt. i. 6; Acts xiii. 22).[1] And Melchizedek, as King of Salem—of peace and righteousness (Heb. vii. 1-2) is, in the sense of the allegorical interpretation of Scripture, the " type " pointing to Christ.

2. (*a*) Hence it is obvious that in the N.T. it is Jesus Christ who is regarded as *the* King. First, as Messiah, Jesus is *basileus tōn Ioudaiōn* (Matt. ii. 2, xxvii. 11, 29, 37; Mark xv. 2, 9, 12, 18, 26; Luke xxiii. 3, 37 f.; John xviii. 33, 37, 39, xix. 3, 14 f., 19, 21). But this usage is rather changeable. An uninterested contemporary of Jesus like Pilate knows nothing further than to take this title from his Jewish accusers (Luke xxiii. 2 f.). For the obdurate Jewish enemies of Jesus—in this connexion Pharisees and Sadducees go together—the title is a blasphemous claim of the deceitful messianic pretender. In Jewish eyes Jesus is a man who makes Himself a king (John xix. 12). The fickle mob, sensing but not understanding the messianic claims of Jesus—in whose ranks are to be found disciples in the school of Jesus—misinterpret the term " king of the Jews " more or less politically. The people want to make Jesus king, and do not perceive what they are actually about (John vi. 15). In a word, the fact that Jesus is designated as king merges into the messianic problem which is the very essence of Jesus' messiahship. If the messianic claim actually bound up with the royal title is to be underlined then Israel must be named instead of the Jews. In fact we also find—if but relatively seldom—the title *basileus* (*tou*) *Israēl* (Matt. xxvii. 42; Mark xv. 32; John i. 49, xii. 13). In any

[1] The difficult passage about the Davidic sonship (Mark xii. 35-7, and parallels) makes no difference in this connexion.

case, the Jew who knew of the promises given to his
people was bound to speak of the King of Israel. To
the daughter of Zion, as the true Israel, comes the
promise of Zech. ix. 9; " See thy King comes to thee "
(Matt. xxi. 5; John xii. 15). This Messiah-King, at
God's behest, conducts the final judgement (Matt. xxv.
34, 40). According to Ps. cxviii. 26, Jesus, at His entry
into Jerusalem, is the blessed King who comes in the
name of the Lord (Luke xix. 38). Only so is Jesus the
Messiah-King (*Christos basileūs*), who stands in contrast
to the Roman Emperor, a contrast misunderstood by
Jews and Gentiles (Luke xxiii. 2).[1] It seems at first
sight remarkable that, apart from the Evangelists, the
individual N.T. authors use neither " King of the Jews "
nor " King of Israel " of Jesus. The designations are
absent from the earliest *kerugma* as we find it in Acts, and
also from St. Paul. To deduce from this that the
original Christian community, to whom the evangelists
also belonged, did not know or use the missing designations would be unconvincing. A hidden proof that
the royal title for Jesus was also not alien to the *kerugma*
can be found in Acts xvii. 7, where the Jews in Thes-
salonica denounce the Christians for high treason, for
maintaining that another was king, namely Jesus. At
the same time the marked reticence is revealing. We
may conjecture that the difficulty about the messiahship
of Jesus of Nazareth, already referred to as the messianic
problem, brought with it a certain uncertainty and

---

[1] On the subject of these contrasts within the framework of the
messianic secret much material is provided by the comprehensive
study by R. Eisler, Ἰησοῦς βασιλεὺς οὐ βασιλεύσας (1924-30),
esp. ii, pp. 374 and 688, with his acute, but often obscure and
unreliable detailed hypotheses. Eisler is criticised by H. Win-
disch, *Gnomon*, vii (1931), pp. 289-307. H. Lewy, *Deutsche
Literaturzeitung*, 21 (1930), pp. 481-94, and W. Windfuhr, *Philol.
Wochenschrift*, liii (1933), pp. 9 ff. [An English résumé of his
theories appeared in 1931, *The Messiah Jesus and John the Baptist.*]

therefore reticence. The situation also provides us with the evidence that the whole complex of the messianic secret, not properly comprehended by the first Christian community, is a vital component of the history of the Christ upon earth, that Jesus Himself, as the King of the Jews (or of Israel), regarded Himself as the Messiah of His people. The fourth evangelist here agrees entirely with the others, except that he goes further in the answer to Pilate's questioning by giving a christological definition of the Kingship of Jesus (John xviii. 37). The Book of Revelation takes up a special point of view in raising the royal title into a cosmological term. The eschatological messianic King bears sway over the entire universe. In the so-called synoptic apocalypse (part of Mark xiii, and parallels) the situation is the same. Here too fits St. Paul's description of Christ's judgement in 1 Cor. xv. 24, where Christ restores the sovereignty to God (the Father) at the end of time. In this sense is Jesus Christ (in 1 Tim. vi. 15—corresponding to the hymnodic style of Revelation) King of Kings and Lord of Lords.

In the Apostolic Fathers Christ is designated *basilēus megas* (Didache xiv. 3 after Malachi i. 14). He is preceded by a messianic-apocalyptic foe (an Antichrist) by a *basilēus mikros* (Epistle of Barnabas iv. 4; cf. Dan. vii. 24). When Christ is called King, it is in connexion with the heightening of the dignity of the incarnate, who is installed as King by God the King (Diognetus vii. 4). With regard to the result, and the ensuing example of the effect of the incarnation, Christ's title of *basilēus* is enlarged by the addition of the attribute *sōsas* (Polycarp ix. 3) and the title *didaskalos* (*ib*. xvii. 3).

(*b*) When the sovereignty is given back by His Christ to God, then St. Paul thinks of *God the Father as the eternal King*. This is clearly expressed in 1 Tim. i.

17 where God is *basilēus tōn aiōnōn* (cf. Tobit xiii. 6, 10). For the rest, there is only one passage in Matt. (v. 35), where God is praised as the *megas basilēus*. It is noticeable that it is the First Evangelist, so specially rooted in the O.T., who includes this reference. It follows that he also passes down to us more parables of God's Kingdom than the other evangelists. And in some of these parables God is King in His diverse functions: cf. Matt. xiv. 9, xviii. 23, xxii. 2, 7, 11, 13.

The Apostolic Fathers, naturally, like the philosophically influenced Judaism of the Diaspora, include a greater variety of epithets for God than 'does the N.T. As in 1 Tim. i. 17, a passage which belongs even more closely to the sphere just described, so in 1 Clement lxi. 2, God is named *basilēus tōn aiōnōn* and praised as *despotēs epouranios*. In Hermas v. 3, 9, 8, God is *ho basilēus ho megas;* cf. Ps. xlvii. 3 (in lxx) and Tobit xiii. 15. God is *basilēus* also in Diognetus vii. 4.

(*c*) According to the not specially well-attested readings in Rev. i. 6, and v. 10, *Christians* also can be called *basileis*.[1] In any case the verbs *basilēuō* and *sumbasilēuō* are used of Christians.

B. BASILEIA [2]

1. *Its basic meaning*

As to the general use of this term, it must be said that the word, which we mostly translate as *kingdom, realm*, originally means only the *being, essence, situation,*

---

[1] A formal analogy to this transferred (inappropriate) use of *basilēus* in the sense of someone who stands out from other people occurs in Philostratus Vitae Sophistarum ii. 10, 2, where Herodes Atticus occurs as *ho basileus tōn logōn*.

[2] Beside the expositions of Holstein and Gloege (see Bibliography, p. xi), it must be mentioned that an examination, in method lexicographical, and true to the texts—as is here undertaken by way of acceptance and deepening of the article in

of a king. As it is a question of a king, we do best to speak of his *dignity*, his *power*. That is true of the earliest example of the word—τὴν βασιληίην (Ionian for *basileian*) ἔχε τὴν Λυδῶν (Herodotus i. 11). So also Xenophon *Memorabilia*, iv. 6, 12: βασιλείαν . . . καὶ τυραννίδα ἀρχὰς μὲν ἀμφοτέρας ἡγεῖτο εἶναι, διαφέρειν δὲ ἀλλήλων ἐνόμιζε (cf. the difference between *basileus* and *turannos* p. 1, note 2). Inevitably an often-found second meaning follows: the dignity of a king shows itself in the *territory* ruled over by him, in his *realm.*[1] Such a change of meaning is clear in the word " dukedom " and in the more general term " empire ". In kingship, on the other hand, the secondary meaning has not established itself, but the original meaning of the ending -ship, referring to position and dignity, has remained predominant. In *basileia* both meanings are present. In Rev. xvii. 12 and xvii. 17, the double sense seems to be indissolubly present.[2]

A survey of the O.T. (Hebrew and Aramaic and LXX; cf. supra pp. 4 ff.) of the Pseudepigrapha and Apocalyptic literature (with the rabbinic literature pp. 15 ff.) and the other hellenistic writers (above all, Philo: supra pp. 22 ff.) shows that the meaning *status*, or

---

H. Cremer's *Biblisch-theologisch Wörterbuch des N.T. griechisch*, 11th edn., revised by J. Kögel (1923)—is of special value for the examination of theological questions in the Bible. Questionable modern categories such as " dynamic ", " ultratemporality ", " anti-secularism " (especially used by Gloege) should be avoided. Exegesis should, moreover, not stand aside from the long struggle about the immanence and transcendence of the Kingdom of God—a struggle that has proved fruitless and was bound to do so—as may happen if it uses a newer, possibly better, terminology in contrast to one older and less good.

[1] Well explained by Suidas, s.v.: τὸ ἀξίωμα καὶ τὸ ἔθνος βασιλευόμενον.

[2] In modern Greek *basileia* means " monarchy ", " royal rule ", also " duration of reign "; for " royal realm ", *basileion* is used.

power, is in the foreground. For the N.T. too, this basic meaning is decisive.[1]

2. *The earthly Basileia*

(*a*) To the earthly *basileūs* (cf. pp. 1 ff.) corresponds the earthly *basileia* as monarchy or King's realm. The two meanings established in the introduction are interwoven, but in some N.T. passages can be separated, according to the context. When in the Parable of the Pounds we hear of a pre-eminent man who is reported to have travelled to a distant land *labein heautōi basileian* and returned *labonta tēn basileian* (Luke xix. 12, 15), on both occasions it is a question of *royal status*.[2] The same verbal link is found in Rev. xvii. 12: *deka basileis . . . basileian . . . oupō elabon*.[3] To this fits the next passage Rev. xvii. 17: *dounai ten basileian tōi thēriōi* [3] and Rev. xvii. 18: *hē polis hē megalē hē echousa basileian epi tōn basileōn tēs gēs*.[4] In other N.T. passages the meaning *King's realm* is natural. Thus Matt. iv. 8 = Luke iv. 5, where the Devil at the temptation of Jesus shows him " all the kingdoms of the world ". From the fact that the plural is used and something visible displayed, the meaning " royal realm " or just " realm " follows naturally.[5] When Jesus in his

[1] Cf. some English statements: A. E. J. Rawlinson, *The Gospel according to St. Mark* (1925), p. 111, speaks of " God's Rule or Sovereignty, the Reign of God "; A. Deissmann, *The Religion of Jesus and the Faith of Paul* (1923), pp. 108 ff., " Kingdom or sovereignty, kingly rule of God "; J. Warschauer, *The historical Life of Christ* (1927), " What we translate ' the Kingdom of God ' means thus rather His ' Kingship ', His ' reign ' rather than His ' realm '."

[2] So e.g. E. Klostermann, *Lukasevangelium* (1929), *ad loc.*

[3] E. Lohmeyer, *Apokolypse* (1926), *ad loc.* " monarchy ".

[4] Freely translated, op. cit., " The great city is queen over the kings of the earth ".

[5] Klostermann's *Matthäusevangelium* and *Lukasevangelium*, *ad loc.*, " Realms (*Reiche*) of the world ".

defence against the Pharisees says "πᾶσα βασιλεία μερισ-
θεῖσα καθ' ἑαυτῆς ἐρημοῦται" (Matt. xii. 25; Mark
iii. 24, and Luke xi. 17 are similar), the predicative
verb and the conjunction with a *polis* or an *oikia* (*oikos*)
indicate the translation " royal realm ". When we
find in the apocalyptic speech of Jesus " *egerthēsetai
ethnos ep' ethnos kai basileia epi basileian*" (Matt. xxiv. 7,
and parallels) the connexion with *ethnos* points to the
meaning *royal realm*. The same is true when the
tetrarch Herod promises his daughter " *heōs hēmisous
tēs basileias mou* " (Mark vi. 23) and in *egeneto hē basileia
autou* (sc. *tou thēriou*) *eskotōmene* (Rev. xvi. 10).

This sort of earthly *basileia* carries with it the circumstance that the contrast to, or at least the subjection
under, the *basileia* of God gets emphasised, just as the
kosmos (Matt. iv. 8 or the *oikoumenē* (Luke iv. 5) as the
basileia tou kosmou (Rev. xi. 15) is against God, because
it has sold its soul to the " Anti-King ", i.e. the Devil.
A special feature of this is the fact that the apocalyp-
tically interpreted (i.e. recognised as devilish) World-
power of the *imperium romanum* (the *thērion* in Revelation!) wishes to set up the *basileia* and so diffuse light
where it nevertheless lies in wickedness and deceit in
darkness (*eskotōmenē* Rev. xvi. 10). That the Devil
claims to have a *basileia* follows from the facts that he,
as tempter, leads astray the *basileiai* of the world, and
that Jesus in speaking *vis-à-vis* the Pharisees in general
of an earthly *basileia* directs his words especially to the
basileia of the Devil.

(*b*) In the framework of this apologetic discourse the
phrase " the Devil's *basileia* " is actually used: πῶς
οὖν σταθήσεται ἡ βασιλεία αὐτοῦ (sc. τοῦ σατανᾶ). This
can mean either royal realm, or status (Matt. xii. 26
= Luke xi. 18).

(*c*) Over against such an earthly-human, in the last
resort devilish, *basileia* stands the *basileia* of the men

4

chosen by God and the people chosen by him. Legitimate proprietor, indeed representative, of the *basileia* is King David ; εὐλογημένη ἡ ἐρχομένη βασιλεία τοῦ πατρὸς ἡμῶν Δαυίδ (Mark xi. 10). It is only to Israel as the people of God of the Old and New Covenant (*Israel kata pneuma*) that the *basileia* belongs, for which Christ's disciples are asking and hoping : κύριε, εἰ ἐν τῷ χρόνῳ τούτῳ ἀποκαθιστάνεις τὴν βασιλείαν τῷ Ἰσραήλ; (Acts i. 6).[1]

3. *The Basileia of Christ*

Since, as has been shown above, Jesus Christ is in the N.T. (based on O.T.) the King of the true Israel, we find also mention of the *basileia* of Christ. The " Son of Man " will send out his angels, and they will collect *ek tēs basileias autou* all deceivers and evildoers (Matt. xiii. 41). Jesus says, " There are some standing here who shall not taste death until they see the ' Son of Man ' coming ἐν τῇ βασιλείᾳ αὐτοῦ " (Matt. xvi. 28). Of Jesus Christ as King we read *tēs basileias autou* there shall be no end (Luke i. 33). To his disciples this King promises " you shall eat and drink ἐν τῇ βασιλείᾳ μου " (Luke xxii. 30). To the suffering and dying Messiah-King His fellow-victim of crucifixion cries " Remember me when Thou comest εἰς τὴν βασιλείαν σου " (other reading : ἐν τῇ βασιλείᾳ σου : Luke xxiii. 42). Of the nature of His Kingdom Jesus says " *hē basileia hē emē* is not of this world " (John xviii. 36). The apostle of Christ tells of τὴν ἐπιφάνειαν αὐτοῦ καὶ τὴν βασιλείαν αὐτοῦ (2 Tim. iv. 1). He knows that his Lord will deliver him *eis tēn basileian autou ten epouranion* (2 Tim. iv. 18). To us Christians is granted the entrance *eis*

[1 Many scholars, however, would stress that these two references to the return of David's and Israel's, *basileia* do not represent the mind of Jesus Himself.]

tēn aiōnion basileian tou kuriou hemōn kai soteros Iesou Christou (2 Peter i. 11).

This *basileia* of Jesus Christ is at the same time the *basileia* of God. In various passages we find mention of the Kingdom of God *and* Christ. The unbeliever has no inheritance *en tei basileiai tou Christou kai theou* (Eph. v. 5). At the end of time the *basileia tou kosmou* becomes that of our Lord and His Anointed—τοῦ κυρίου ἡμῶν καὶ τοῦ χριστοῦ αὐτοῦ (Rev. xi. 15). Thus God and Christ stand side by side, now God, now Christ, being mentioned first. It is therefore certain that there can be no question of the *basileia* of Christ being mentioned apart from that of God. Jesus Himself says " My Father has bequeathed to me a *basileian* (Luke xx. 29). It is God who has delivered us unto the *basileian tou huiou tēs agapēs autou* (Col. i. 13). At the end of time Christ, who has similarly received the *basileia* from the Father, gives it back to Him (1 Cor. xv. 24). He can give to God only that which is already His own. And so we pass to consider the expression *basileia (tou) theou*, which dominates the entire N.T., about which is here already spoken implicitly in the foregoing pages; in what follows we shall at the same time have to speak explicitly also about the *basileia (tou) Christou*.

4. *The Basileia of God*

(a) *The terminology.* In surveying the terminology of the " Reich " (Kingdom) of God there are four main divisions: the juxtaposition of *basileia tou theou* and *basileia tōn ouranōn;* *basileia* used absolutely; attributive and predicative statements; synonyms.

The expression *basileia tōn ouranōn*, " Kingdom of Heaven ", is only found in Matthew in the N.T. except for the textually uncertain passage, John iii. 5; outside it also, and significantly, in the Gospel according to the Hebrews fr. 11 (*regnum coelorum*). Furthermore, Matthew has the phrase *basileia tou theou*, God's Kingdom, generally found in Mark, Luke and elsewhere, certainly three times—Matt. xii. 28, xxi. 31, xxi. 43—and probably also a fourth time (Matt. vi. 33, where, it is true, *tou theou* is not in all the manuscripts), and possibly also a fifth time, if *tōn ouranōn* is not the correct reading, in Matt. xix. 24. The question arises, why this double terminology in Matthew? Did the First Evangelist make a distinction between his generally used *tōn ouranōn* and his less frequent *tou theou?* In general one must come to the conclusion that, as the manuscripts and synoptic parallel passages change about between both phrases, they are used indifferently and mean the same. Whether Jesus Himself used one or the other term in Aramaic, remains disputed. It might be maintained that " Kingdom of Heaven " has a special significance in that by it is meant the power that comes from Heaven [1] and enters into the world. Thereby we gain two important insights. We see again, and clearly, that the essential meaning is not realm, but *sway*. Bound up with this is the realisation that such a power of Heaven can from its very nature not connote a Kingdom that comes about as a result of a natural development of earthly relationships or human strivings, but through an intervention of God from Heaven. As, moreover, in late Jewish speech the word " God " can be replaced by " Heaven ", it follows that the phrase *basileia tou theou* means precisely the same as *basileia tōn ouranōn*. Not different is the expression *basileia tou patros*, " Kingdom of the Father ", Matt. xiii. 43, xxvi. 29. Cf. also Matt. vi. 10 (" May thy, our father's, Kingdom come ") and Matt. xxv. 34 and Luke xii. 32 (" it has pleased your father to give you the Kingdom ").

[1] The plural is a semitism. Contrast 2 Cor. xii. 2.

A large number of passages speak of the *basileia* without any qualification, i.e. absolutely: Matt. iv. 23, ix. 35, xiii. 19, xxiv. 14 (*euangellion*, or *logos tēs basileias* viii. 12, xiii. 38 (*huioi tēs basileias*), Heb. xi. 33 (*dia pisteōs katēgōnisanto basileiās*), xii. 28 (*basileian asaleuton paralambanontes*), James ii. 5 (*klēronomous tēs basileiās*); perhaps also Acts xx. 25 (*kerussōn tēn basileiān*).[1] There is no need to prove that in all these passages the Kingdom of God is in mind, as is made certain by the contexts and by special attributes and predicates.[2]

Since any qualifications, whether expressed (by the addition of *tou theou*, *tōn ouranōn*) or not (used absolutely), are bound up with the Being and Acts of God, further direct attributes are very rare. Besides the already mentioned Heb. xii. 38 (*asaleutos*), there is also 1 Tim. iv. 18 (*epouranios*) and 2 Peter i. 11 (*aiōnios*). In the case of other aspects of God's Kingdom, other such attributes are more rhetorical and formal rather than realistically theological in their effect. The N.T. has also but few direct predicates. Whose is the *basileia tou theou?* Obviously God's—and men's, but only those men who are poor (in spirit) (Matt. v. 3; Luke vi. 20), who are persecuted for righteousness' sake (Matt. v. 10).

More detailed attributive and predicative statements bring us into a complex range of synonyms calculated to make clear the complexity of the proclamation of God's Kingdom. It makes no difference whether synonymous phrases are tacked on with an " and " (hendiadys) or whether they occur as predicates. It

[1] To which many manuscripts add *tou* (*kuriou*) *Iēsou*, or *tou theou*.

[2] This absolute use has led to a religious or religious-sounding, but really immanent-secular and pseudo-theological, use of the term realm (*Reich*). Cf. Religious-Socialism or the *dritte Reich* of the Nazis (linked with the faith in the old " Holy Roman Empire "—which in its turn looks back to the absolute use of *basileia*).

makes no difference in what order such expressions come, or in what order they are treated here. It is always a question of the many-sided and yet clear Being and Acting of God, and His call to and claims upon, men. Men are to seek God's Kingdom and His righteousness (Matt. vi. 33). This righteousness and peace and " joy in the Holy Spirit " build up the Kingdom of God (Rom. xiv. 17). This all means no innate, acquired or " to be acquired " quality, but is *palingenesia* ("being born again ")—the word used in Matt. xix. 28 (cf. John iii. 3 ff.), whereas the parallel passage in Luke xxii. 30, has *basileia*. In this connexion the writer of Revelation speaks to his brother-Christians as their brother and companion ἐν τῇ θλίψει καὶ βασιλείᾳ καὶ ὑπομονῇ ἐν Ἰησοῦ (Rev. i. 9). To him has come ἡ σωτηρία καὶ ἡ δύναμις καὶ ἡ βασιλεία τοῦ Θεοῦ ἡμῶν καὶ ἡ ἐξουσία τοῦ χριστοῦ αὐτοῦ (Rev. xii. 10). Such a power (*dunamis*) of God is also spoken of when something like a definition of God's Kingdom has to be given. God's Kingdom comes *en dunamei* (Mark ix. 1); it does not exist *en logōi* (of men) but *en dunamei* (of God) (1 Cor. iv. 20).[1] Alternatively, to the Kingdom of God comes *doxa*—the glory of God (1 Thess. ii. 12); indeed *doxa* and *basileia* can be changed over, as Mark x. 37 shows with ἐν τῇ δόξῃ σου where the parallel passage in Matt. xx. 21 has ἐν τῇ βασιλείᾳ σου. The realm of Christ as sent from God coincides with His *epiphaneia* (2 Tim. iv. 1). Such a *basileia asaleutos* is for the believers grace (*charis*) (Heb. xii. 38); it is

[1] This Pauline passage would be entirely misunderstood if one were to see here only the well-known antithesis between word and deed, between talking and acting. The point here is that human work has no value *vis-à-vis* God's power. The following paraphrase gets the point: " Not in human deeds but in God's word is the Kingdom of God." The whole emphasis is on God's Kingdom, as the sovereign, unambiguous, logical subject of the sentence.

epangelia, as the manuscripts ℵ and A read for *basileia* in James ii. 5; it is life (*zoē*) into which one enters as into the Kingdom of God (Matt. xviii. 9) whereas in the parallel passage, Mark ix. 47, the text has *basileia*. The Scribes and Pharisees have wished to exclude from this Kingdom a man whom God has admitted to His Kingdom (Matt. xxiii. 13), replaced by the " keys of knowledge " (*gnōsis*) in the parallel passage Luke xi. 52; thus *basileia* (*theou*) is even the same as *gnosis* (*theou*)!

All these synonyms show that God's *basileia*, meaning God's ways with men, constitutes a soteriological entity, of which the explanation stands or falls with that of the general soteriology in the preaching of Jesus Christ and His apostles.

(*b*) The last sentence also means that in the Kingdom of God we are concerned with the entire preaching of Jesus Christ and His apostles. If the entire proclamation of the N.T. is *euangelion*, then this is the *euangelion* of God's Kingdom. For *euangelion tou theou* in Mark i. 14 many manuscripts read *euangelion tēs basileiās tou theou*. This summarising passage corresponds to other similar passages such as Matt. iv. 23, ix. 35; cf. also xxiv. 14. The verb *euangelizesthai* also refers to God's reign—Luke iv. 43, viii. 1, xvi. 16; Acts viii. 12. The same is the message of cognate verbs like *kērussein* (Matt. iv. 23, ix. 35; Luke ix. 2; Acts xx. 25, xxviii. 31), or *diamarturesthai* (Acts xxviii. 23), or *diangellein* (Luke ix. 60), or *peithein* (Acts xix. 8), or *lalein* (Luke ix. 11), or finally *legein* (Acts i. 3). As the *euangelion* of God's Kingdom, so also mention is made of the *mustērion* (or the plural *mustēria* = revelation!) of God's Kingdom (Matt. xiii. 11 and parallels) or the *logos* of God's Kingdom (Matt. xiii. 19) whereas in the parallel passages Mark iv. 15 and Luke viii. 12, we find *logos* alone, meaning the " word of God ". The whole of such preaching is expressly secured through the much-stressed binding of word and deed in decisive passages.   Together with the direction to His disciples to proclaim God's Kingdom Jesus gives also the direction to heal the sick (Luke ix. 2; cf. Matt. x. 7 f.; Mark iii. 13 f.) Jesus sees in the fact that he expels demons the breaking in of God's Kingdom (Matt. xii. 28 = Luke xi. 20).   Thus from this point there is not only the word of God's Kingdom, but, coinciding with it, the deeds of God's sovereignty.   That is expressly emphasised in the summaries by the evangelists (tacked on to the oldest *kērugma*); cf. Matt. iv. 23.

(*c*) What is the point of impact for this N.T. proclamation?   Jesus of Nazareth is not the first who has spoken of God's Kingdom, nor John the Baptist.   The preaching of both does not say " I proclaim unto you that there is a Kingdom of God and it looks like so and so " but rather " I proclaim unto you that the Kingdom of God is nigh ".   The theme is thus well known to its first hearers, the Jewish contemporaries.   This concrete link with the situation is decisive.   The positive link for the Baptist and for Jesus is given in the apocalyptic and the rabbinic literature, partly agreeing with, partly differing from each of these two themselves differing movements, which on their part derive originally from the prophets of the O.T.   Details of these may be read in the articles on the O.T. and rabbinic periods, which are here presupposed.   For the N.T. authors, naturally writing in Greek, the Greek translations of the O.T. are of importance.   When in Heb. i. 8, in the middle of a long O.T. quotation, mention is made of the ῥάβδος τῆς βασιλείας αὐτοῦ (LXX σου) it is a question of the use of Ps. xliv. 7, out of the Septuagint.[1]   On the other hand there are, in the

---

[1] The writer of Heb. argues entirely on the basis of LXX, writing the " best " Greek of the New Testament.   [The Hebrew—Psalm xlv. 7—speaks of a sceptre.]

LXX, as we have seen, some specifically hellenistic passages; these are not of importance as a point of contact for the N.T. proclamation of the " Kingdom of God ". The same is true of Philo and Josephus.

(*d*) If the " Kingdom of God " as has been shown from the terminology, means the existence of royal sovereignty, that is confirmed fully when we examine the details of the contexts. The most important statement is that the Kingdom of God is near, has drawn near, has come to us, is coming, will manifest itself, shall come: ἤγγικεν [1] (Matt. iii. 2, iv. 17 = Mark i. 15; Matt. x. 7; Luke x. 9, 11), ἐγγύς ἐστιν (Luke xxi. 31), ἐρχομένη (Mark xi. 10), ἔρχεται (Luke xvii. 20), ἔφθασεν (Matt. xii. 28 = Luke xi. 20), μέλλει ἀποφαίνεσθαι (Luke xix. 11), ἐλθάτω (Matt. vi. 10 = Luke xi. 2).

In the proclamation of Jesus of Nazareth to His disciples (which links closely on to that of John the Baptist), the nature of God's sovereignty is negatively and positively defined, and first and foremost negatively —and precisely thereby positively.[2]

Negatively, the Kingdom of God is contrasted with everything present and earthly, everything now and here; and thus it is something entirely miraculous. And yet somehow it is impossible to interpret God's Kingdom as a *summum bonum*, towards which man strives to reach, to which one can come gradually nearer. From the clue provided at the beginning of

[[1] C. H. Dodd in the *Parables of the Kingdom* (Nisbet), pp. 44 ff, maintains that this too means " has drawn nigh "—right up to us, rather than near at hand.]

[2] For what follows cf. R. Bultmann, *Jesus* (1926), pp. 28-54; K. L. Schmidt, *Jesus Christus*, in RGG., iii (2nd edn.), pp. 129-32; K. L. Schmidt, *Das überweltliche Reich Gottes in der Verkündigung Jesu*, Theolog. *Blätter*, vi (1927), pp. 118-20; K. L. Schmidt, *Die Verkündigung des Neuen Testaments in ihrer Einheit und Besonderheit*, Theolog. *Blätter*, x (1931), pp. 113 ff.

the reported proclamation of the gospel in the words
" μετανοεῖτε · ἤγγικεν γὰρ ἡ βασιλεία τῶν οὐρανῶν "
(Matt. iv. 17), may be seen the supreme question which
is inevitably at stake.   The question is not whether and
how we men can possess the Kingdom of God as a
sentiment in our hearts, whether we men as a fellowship
of disposition can " represent " the Kingdom of God.
For the Kingdom of God comes *to* us, and does so
without our help, without our actions.   But then comes
the question whether or not we belong to this Kingdom
of God.   To desire to attract the Kingdom of God to
ourselves is human precocity, self-justifying Pharisaism,
refined—zealotry!   Thus the hardest thing which is
demanded from men is patience, through which alone
the necessary condition for God's action is guaranteed.
The situation is thus as described in the preaching of
St. Paul, for whom soberness and " quenching not the
spirit " coincide (1 Thess. v. 8, 19).   The Parables of
the Kingdom were spoken to hammer home precisely
this point.   He who cannot show patience in being
" open " for God is like the man who sows seed and
then, like an impatient, inquisitive, child, will not
allow the seed—that grows he knows not how—to grow
up in silence (Parable of the self-growing seed, Mark
iv. 26-9).   Nothing less than a miracle is happening
before our eyes when, without our help, even without
our understanding, out of the smallest grain of seed,
the fruitbearing bush has grown.   That modern man
breaks up this miracle has nothing to do with the
tertium comparationis, which is decisive here.   The
Parables of the Mustard Seed (Matt. xiii. 31 f. and
parallels) and of the Leaven (Matt. xiii. 33 = Luke
xiii. 20 f.) are saying exactly the same.   The same
meaning rather more deeply hidden is to be found in
the other Parables of the Kingdom—only in these a
further point about which we shall speak later is also

playing its part—the Tares (Matt. xiii. 24-30), the Treasure in the Field (Matt. xiii. 44), the Pearl of great price (Matt. xiii. 45 f.), the Fishnet (Matt. xiii. 47-50), the Wicked Servant (Matt. xviii. 23-35), the Labourers in the Vineyard (Matt. xx. 1-16), the Wedding Feast (Matt. xxii. 2-13), the Ten Virgins (Matt. xxv. 1-13). The object of all these parables is to make clear that the ordering of God's Kingdom is different from ordinary human order, that the Kingdom of God is unaccountably, overwhelmingly present among the clues provided by the works of Jesus Christ.

Positively, this Kingdom of God is a cosmic catastrophe which shows itself in certain events such as comprise the eschatological drama of the Jewish Apocalypses. Jesus stands among those of His Jewish contemporaries who have not sold their souls to the day-dreams of a political Messiah, but were waiting for the " Son of Man " coming in the clouds of Heaven (Dan. vii. 13). We must reckon with the possibility that in this context many details (above all in the so-called Synoptic Apocalypse, Mark xiii and parallels) have crept in from the community intoxicated with apocalyptic imagery. But in fact Jesus spoke of eating and drinking in the Kingdom of God (Mark xiv. 25 and parallels). But the decisive point is not that Jesus here shared the conceptions of His contemporaries, still less went further than them. The decisive point is really that in this respect He stopped short of His contemporaries and did so deliberately. In contrast to the genuine Jewish and early Christian apocalyptic He declined to paint pictures of the last things or to calculate the signs of their coming. The scorn of the Sadducees, who put before Him a problem arising from the apocalyptic and resurrection hopes which they themselves (in contrast to the Pharisees) rejected,

failed to touch Him (Mark xii. 25 f.). Of special
clarity is His rejection of all attempts to reckon up the
future. In the passage peculiar to St. Luke (Luke
xvii. 20 f.) we find that " the Kingdom of God does not
come in such a way that one can assess its presence "—
Luther translates here the *ou meta paratēreseōs* freely but
aptly " not with external gestures "—" and one cannot
say ' see here, or there '; for behold the Kingdom of
God is in your midst "—Luther translates here the
entos humōn, wrongly, " inside you ".

The whole point of this much-discussed and sorely
vexed passage is to be found in its rejection of the
contemplation of the signs of the future. The question
whether there is any stress here upon the Kingdom of
God being already present (immanent) at the speaking
of this text is not the point at issue—for one thing in the
aramaic original there is no word for " is " or " will
be ". It is also worth remembering that the syriac
translation demands a re-translation of the Greek word
entos into the cognate aramaic which means " in the
midst of you ". This agrees with the statement of
Jesus about the time of the day of the " Son of Man "
(Matt. xxiv. 26 f.; cf. Luke xvii. 23 f.). Those who
surrounded Jesus often thought differently about the
tokens and essence of the Kingdom of God. Thus the
Sons of Zebedee, or their mother, asked after the best
positions in God's Kingdom, and Jesus answered that
this was a matter for God alone (Mark x. 40 = Matt. xx.
23). The apostolic proclamation of St. Paul, however,
agrees entirely with Jesus; cf. Rom. xiv. 17—" The
Kingdom of God consists not in eating and drinking,
etc."

There is also another point in which Jesus lags
behind the thought-development of His Jewish contemporaries. Although national political hopes for
the future do not stand in the forefront of His thoughts,

where rather salvation for the whole world is expected
from the end of time, yet in many passages the thought
of a preferential place for the Jewish people remains
important; Israel shall and will stand up anew in her
ancient glory: her scattered people will stream together
to the new Jerusalem along with the Gentiles. This
hope is shared by Jesus. He confers upon his disciples,
the "twelve", as the representatives of the twelve
tribes of the people of God, of the Holy People, the
office of judges and rulers in the Kingdom of God
(Matt. xix. 28 = Luke xx. 29 f.). But, like the
Baptist, Jesus also stresses in this very point something
negative; the Jew as such has nevertheless no special
claims in the eyes of God; for he can and will, on the
Judgement Day, be ashamed, even before the heathen.
This rôle of Israel is conceived as it was afterwards by
St. Paul (Rom. ii: the rejection of Israel; Rom. ix-xi:
the salvation of Israel). Such care for the people of
Israel is in no sense pointed against Rome. On this
point the Jewish *Shemone Esra*, with its patriotic national
strain, must be set beside the Lord's Prayer, with its
setting of limits to the patriotic and national. Thus in
the preaching of the Kingdom of God what is immanent
is never proclaimed at the expense of what is transcendent. The Kingdom of God lies beyond ethics.
Whoever concentrates wholly upon ethics centres his
thought logically upon the single individual. But in
the case of Jesus and his apostles it is not the individual
as such who receives the promises, but only the congregation, as a member of which the individual
receives salvation.

This proclamation of the Kingdom of God would be
misunderstood if one were to overlook the contrast
already sketched with Judaism. But it would also be
misunderstood if this contrast were to be understood
from the standpoint of Hellenism. Greek thought, in

which we are so much wrapped up, sees in mankind a developing character, through which what is corporeal and sensuous dies out and what is spiritual grows. But it is also not permissible to replace individualism by universalism. This ideal of mankind is also alien to Jesus and his apostles, however well known it was in late classical philosophy. Whoever regards the N.T. preaching of God's Kingdom in the light of this popular philosophical background is transforming that preaching, and setting in place of human apocalyptic phantasy and human political daydreams nothing further than a refined humanism. But where God breaks into life with His sovereignty, where God speaks and acts, no spiritualism, no mysticism, no ecstasy can prepare access to Him. Such refined human possibilities of a link with God, as Hellenism knows them, are made impossible by the naïver Jewish pictures of Heaven and Hell. Even more than a sublime philosophy, anthropomorphic conceptions of God and His Kingdom leave God as the Lord, untarnished in His transcendent majesty. But here we must remember a yet further consideration: even expressions like " supernaturalism ", " transcendence ", " cosmic catastrophe", " miracles ", become at once inadequate, when men hope to feel at home in a superior world by their aid. The negative point that God's Kingdom is a sheer miracle must be held fast to, in stark negativity. This negative, which sees God's Kingdom as the quite other, the entirely supernatural and anti-secular, is much the most positive statement that could possibly be made. The realisation of God's sovereignty is future. And this future conditions man in the present. To man who is faced with God and His sovereignty comes the call to repentance. Where man listens to this call with faith, i.e. in obedience, then he comes into contact with God's Kingdom, which comes without his doing anything to it; there the gospel becomes a message of glad tidings that strikes home.

(*e*) A many-sided terminology shows in what way man can find himself in contact with God's Kingdom. The fundamental point is that he is " receiving " God's gifts. God gives His Kingdom: " it is the Father's good pleasure to give you the *basileia* " (Luke xii. 32). Jesus Christ promises to Peter as he makes his confession " I will give thee the keys of the Kingdom of Heaven " (Matt. xvi. 19). From the obdurate Jews the Kingdom is taken away and given instead to the faithful—" to a nation which creates the fruits of it " (Matt. xxi. 34). Christ bequeaths the Kingdom, as His Father has bequeathed it to Him: διατίθεμαι ὑμῖν καθὼς διέθετό μοι ὁ πατήρ μου βασιλείαν (Luke xxii. 29). God calls Christians into His Kingdom and into His glory (*doxa*) (1 Thess. ii. 12). God has transferred us into the Kingdom of the Son of His love: μετέστησεν εἰς τὴν βασιλείαν τοῦ υἱοῦ τῆς ἀγάπης αὐτοῦ (Col. i. 13). The faithful are made worthy of the Kingdom of God: καταξιωθῆναι ὑμῖς τῆς βασιλείας τοῦ θεοῦ (2 Thess. i. 5). The Lord will deliver the faithful into His Heavenly Kingdom; . . . ῥύσεταί με ὁ κύριος . . . σώσει εἰς τὴν β. αὐτοῦ τὴν ἐπουράνιον (2 Tim. iv. 18). God has promised His Kingdom: ἐπηγγείλετο (Jas. ii. 5). God does not behave as do the Pharisees, who take it upon themselves to bar the Kingdom from men: οὐαὶ . . . ὅτι κλείετε τὴν β. τῶν οὐρανῶν ἔμπροσθεν τῶν ἀνθρώπων (Matt. xxiii. 13; cf. Luke xi. 52).

To these expressions correspond various correlatives on the side of the believing man. He *receives* God's Kingdom as a child: ὅς ἂν μὴ δέξηται τὴν β. τοῦ θεοῦ ὡς παιδίον (Mark x. 15 = Luke xviii. 17). Joseph of Arimathea is in the situation of one *prosdechomonenos tēn basileian tou theou* (Mark xv. 43 = Luke xxiii. 51). *Paralambanein* (Heb. xii. 28), is similar. Especially frequent and, corresponding to the *diathēkē* of God's Kingdom, is the expression *klēronomein* (Matt. xxv. 34; I Cor. vi. 9, 10, xv. 50; Gal. v. 21); similarly *echei klēronomian en tēi basileiāi* (Eph. v. 5) and *klēronomous tēs basileiās* (Jas. ii. 5). To be thus chosen by God means *seeing* God's Kingdom. Some will be chosen to see God's Kingdom before their death (Mark ix. 1 and parallels). Only to him that has been born again will this insight be granted (John iii. 3). Another particularly frequent expression is that of *entering into* God's Kingdom: εἰσέρχεσθαι or also εἰσπορεύεσθαι (Matt. v. 20, vii. 21, xviii. 3 and parallels; xix. 23 f. and parallels; xxiii. 13—cf. Luke xi. 52; Mark ix. 47; John iii. 5; Acts xiv. 22); εἴσοδος (2 Peter i. 11). Next we come to the passages in which the phrase *en tēi basileiāi* is used: Matt. v. 19, viii. 11 = Luke xiii. 28 f.; Matt. xi. 11 = Luke vii. 28; Matt. xiii. 43, xviii. 1, 4, xx. 21, xxvi. 29 and parallels; Luke xiv. 15, xxii. 16, 30, xxiii. 42 (other reading *eis*), Eph. v. 5; Rev. i. 9. Before the self-righteous Pharisees, publicans and harlots have access into God's Kingdom: προάγουσιν ὑμᾶς εἰς τὴν β. (Matt. xxi. 31). The Jews should be *huioi tēs basileiās* (Matt. viii. 12), but as a result of their stubbornness they are not (cf. Matt. xiii. 38). The Scribe who is busy about the things of God is *ou makran apo tēs basileias tou theou* (Mark xii. 34). The true scribe, as God would have him, is *mathēteutheis tēi b. tōn ouranōn* (Matt. xiii. 52). Whoever really decides for God is *enthetos* (fit for) *tēi b. tou theou* (Luke ix. 62). When that is so, at the same moment comes the appeal to busy oneself properly over the things of God. We are to be like St. Paul's *sunergoi* (fellow-workers) *eis* [towards] *tēn b. tou theou* (Col. iv. 11). One must take care to notice that the phrase here is not *sunergoi tēs basileiās.* . . . Thus in spite of this expression it is not a case of synergism.

Thus, as faith is obedience towards God's commandments, so now there is demanded of us effort and striving. Through faith we are to fight for God's Kingdom like the chosen people of the Old Covenant: *dia pisteōs katēgōnisanto basileiās* (Heb. xi. 33). In a word, we are to seek after God's sovereignty, to *look* for it; *Zēteite . . . prōton tēn basileian* (Matt. vi. 33 = Luke xii. 31). This *zētein* is something different from *biazesthai* [use violence to] and *harpazein* [snatch] (Matt. xi. 12 = Luke xvi. 15).

To whom then does God's Kingdom belong? To whom will it be given? To whom has it been promised? To those who are poor (in spirit) (Matt. v. 3 = Luke vi. 20), to those who (Matt. v. 10) are persecuted for righteousness' sake! To children! (Matt. xix. 14 and parallels). The last-named passages above all make clear how great, how unspeakable is the decision laid upon us. It is a question of accepting invitations into God's Kingdom in *metanoia*, i.e. for His sake to bid farewell to all the other things of this world, riches and worldly fame, in other words, not to behave as did those invited to the Wedding Feast, who excused themselves with various pretexts (Matt. xxii. 1-14 = Luke xiv. 16-24). Once again there are various parables which stress what has been said with special force. For the sake of God's Kingdom, which is like the treasure hid in the field, or the pearl of great price for which a merchant gave all his fortune (Matt. xiii. 44-6), one must pluck out one's eye of temptation or cut off one's tempting hand (Matt. v. 29 f.). The crassest indication comes in the sentence that one must remember that many have made themselves eunuchs for the sake of God's Kingdom (Matt. xix. 12).[1]

[1] This demonstration, in contrast to one or two cases in the early Church (Origen!), should not be understood as a moral injunction but as a shocking, challenging appeal; we are to

In any case the result of a genuine facing of God's kingly power involves the deepest of decisions, the most searching selection of the few from the many (Matt. xxii. 14).[1] A sharp " either-or " demands irrevocable decision: " He who puts his hand to the plough, and looks back, is not fit for the Kingdom of God " (Luke ix. 62). Such a decision is no mere enthusiasm: it will not be made in a moment of intoxication, but is a matter of deliberate, sober consideration. As an architect makes a true estimate before building starts, as a king does not embark upon war without a plan of campaign (Luke xiv. 28-32), so must he who is bidden by God to enter His Kingdom deliberate as to the true acceptance of the summons. He who accepts without making clear to himself the nature of his undertaking, he who hears without due submission, is like the man who builds his house upon sand (Matt. vii. 24-7 = Luke vi. 47-9). Not everyone that says " Lord, Lord " will enter into the Kingdom of Heaven, but only he who does the will of God (Matt. vii. 21). The demand is for sacrifice up to the limit, right up to complete sacrifice of self, to hatred of one's own family (Matt. x. 37 = Luke xiv. 26). Who can really do that? Who ventures so far as to be to that extent submissive to the will of God? Nobody, except for—Jesus Christ Himself!

(*f*) With these words we arrive at the inescapable

reflect that men who have been completely in earnest about God's Kingdom, have now and then taken upon themselves even to go as far as to castrate themselves—which is thereby neither praised nor blamed, at any rate not praised. This interpretation of the difficult saying is surely preferable to the more pedestrian, although not quite impossible explanation, that here and there men have voluntarily refrained from sexual intercourse—as did John the Baptist and Jesus Himself.

[1] Cf. the words about the narrow gate and the broad way (Matt. vii. 13 f. = Luke xiii. 23 f.).

and very special relationship between God's sovereignty and Jesus Christ Himself.   It is not the case that
precisely the same language is used of the Kingdom of
Christ (cf. supra, pp. 36 f.) as of the Kingdom of God,
but rather that certain passages presuppose the
equivalence of the Kingdom of God and Christ.
Whereas in Mark xi. 10 there is praise for " the coming
Kingdom of our father David ", Matt. xxi. 9 and Luke
xix. 38 (which are simply parallel to Mark xi. 9) speak
simply of the person of Jesus Messiah.   Even clearer is
the synoptic comparison of *heneken emou kai heneken tou
euangelliou* (Mark x. 29), *heneka tou emou onomatos* (Matt.
xix. 29) and *heineken tēs basileiās tou theou* (Luke xviii.
29) : the name and message of Jesus Christ, and Jesus
Christ Himself, are equated with the Kingdom of God.
First and foremost, this equation is arrived at by way of
the references to the " Son of Man " as the representative of the " people of God ": whereas Mark ix. 1
(= Luke ix. 27) speaks of the coming of God's Kingdom
in power, the parallel passage in Matt. xvi. 28, speaks
of the " Son of Man " coming in and with his Kingdom.
This " Son of Man " and Lord is awaited by Christians
just as is the Kingdom of God itself: cf. e.g. Matt.
xxv. 1 with Luke xii. 35 f.   Exactly parallel is Acts
viii. 12 (*euangelizomenǭ peri tēs basileias tou theou kai tou
onomatos Iēsou Christou*) with Acts xxviii. 31 (*kērussōn tēn
basileian tou theou kai didaskōn ta peri tou kuriou Iēsou
Christou*.   Similarly there is a parallelism in *hē basileia
tou theou hēmōn kai hē exousia tou Christou autou* in Rev.
xii. 10.   Thus the language testifies to what is already
clear from the general context: Jesus knows that the
inrushing sovereignty of God has come into time and
the world in His own person—what is expressed in the
johannine sentence " *Ho logos sarx egeneto* " (John i. 14).
That which is, and remains, future for the Christian,
that for which he waits, is in Jesus Christ alone a

sēmeron (Luke iv. 21; cf. Matt. xi. 5 f. = Luke vii. 22)
[—a present reality]. Upon this decisive equation of
the Messiah Jesus made flesh, risen, and present in the
Church, with the future Kingdom of God depends the
christological *kērugma*, which sees the sending of the
Messiah as an *hapax*, or *ephapax*, event, as an unique
unrepeatable event—" once for all time ". Christ
apethanen hapax (Rom. vi. 10—cf. Heb. vi. ff. and
1 Pet. iii. 18). If one looks for an expression to
summarise the equation described, the term *autobasileia*,
coined by Origen (*Matthew Commentary*, xiv. 7—on
Matt. xviii. 23) (Lommatzsch iii. p. 283) suggests itself [1]
—without, to be sure, accepting the special interpretation put forward by Origen.[2] Before Origen,
Marcion, in his notorious " *Panchristismus* ",[3] had
written: *In evangelio est dei regnum Christus ipse*
(Tertullian, *Adv. Marcion* iv. 33) (iii, p. 532, 6 f.). Jesus
Christ alone obeyed the law, alone had faith (cf. Phil.
ii. 5 ff.), whereby He both proclaimed the message
of God's Kingdom and at the same time performed the
miracles as the signs of God's Kingdom (Matt. xi. 2 ff.
= Luke vii. 18 ff.).

From all this it becomes intelligible why the apostolic
and post-apostolic Church of the N.T. did not speak
often explicitly of the *basileia tou theou*, but always
implicitly stressed this *basileia* by pointing to the *kurios
Iesous Christos*. It is not the case that the emphasis on
the Church has supplanted Jesus of Nazareth's preaching of the Kingdom of God. Rather is it the case that
in the post-Easter experience of Christ the belief in the
Kingdom of God remained firm.

[1] So P. Feine, *Theologie des N.T.* (1910), p. 100 (5th edn., 1931,
p. 80).
[2] Cf. R. Frick, *Die Geschichte des Reich-Gottes-Gedankens in der alten
Kirche bis zu Origenes und Augustin* (1928), p. 101, note 2.
[3] Cf. A. von Harnack, *Marcion* (1924), pp. 223 ff.

5. *The Basileia and the Church*

However clear and distinct be the N.T. testimony of this *autobasileia* of Jesus Christ, the N.T. none the less understandably stops short of identifying the *basileia tou theou* with the believers in Christ. Only one single passage can be found to suggest this: Christ *epoiēsen hēmas basileian*[1] (Rev. i. 6). It is unnecessary to explain, or prove, that Christians can only be spoken of as being the *basileia* in a derivative sense—albeit derived from Christ.

[1] This text, quoted from the O.T., may safely be accepted rather than the other readings *basileion* or *basileis*.

VI. *BASILEIA* (*TOU THEOU*) IN THE EARLY CHURCH [1]

THE connexion between the texts in the Apostolic Fathers about the Kingdom of God with those in the N.T. starts with the fact that the Fathers quote a few N.T. passages—Matt. v. 3, 10 (Luke vi. 20) in Polycarp, ii. 3; Matt. vi. 10 in the *Didache*, viii. 2; 1 Cor. vi. 9 f in Ignatius, Eph. xvi. 1 Phil. iii. 3, *ad Pol.* v. 3.

The usage of " kingdom " and " kingdom of God " is in general as in the N.T. Besides *basileia theou* we often find *basileia tou Christou* 1 Clem. l. 3, etc.). *Basileia* stands alone in 1 Clem. lxi. 1, 2 Clem. v. 5. There are various expressions for man's relations with it, founded upon the N.T. basis—man receives God's gift. Of God, it is said: *edōkas tēn exousian tēs basileiās* (1 Clem. lxi. 1), etc. Man receives (2 Clem. xii. 1), touches (Barnabas, vii. 11), sees, inherits, dwells in it, is glorified in it, enters into it.

In this usage the Apostolic Fathers [2] agree with the N.T. God's kingdom is promised by the Apostles (1 Clem. xlii. 3). Its final coming is fulfilled in the return of Christ (1 Clem. l. 3). The entry of the Christian depends upon the sacrament (Hermas, *Simil.* ix. 16, 2) and upon good works (2 Clem. vi. 9). The ethical imperative is strongly stressed (2 Clem. xi. 7, Barnabas, xxi. 1) but it is always God who brings in His kingdom. Whereas this all agrees with the N.T. in form and content, there is a difference from it in that the coming of God's kingdom is made dependent upon the behaviour of the congregation; thus in 2 Clem. xii. 2 ff., when the Lord is asked when

---

[1] Cf. *basileūs* in the Apostolic Fathers, supra p. 31.
[2] Cf. R. Frick, op. cit. (p. 54, supra) pp. 27-35.

56

His Kingdom will come, He answers: " when the two shall be one, & the outside as the inside, and the male with the feminine neither male nor female." The apocryphal Egyptian Gospel is similar and typifies the ethicalisation of the conception of God's Kingdom in the direction of an ascetic and dualistic perfectionism. In this, faith and morality are not indeed divorced, but separated; in the list of virtues in the Similitudes of Hermas, ix. 15, 2ff. self-control and other virtues are named after faith.

The Apostolic Fathers are not unanimous in following the N.T.'s clear distinction between Kingdom of God and Church. In Barnabas the Kingdom is purely eschatological and therefore not the Church; in viii, 5 the beginning of Christ's royal sovereignty is placed at His crucifixion, and there is an almost chiliastic mention of days of struggle and misfortune even in the Kingdom of Christ. In the *Didache* the Communion Prayers make a clear distinction between the Kingdom of God and the Church, and speak of the *ecclesia* which Christ is collecting up into His Kingdom, but 2 Clem. xiv. 3 says that the Church must be received all at once, exactly as the Kingdom of God. Similarly in Hermas the terms Church and Kingdom of God are very much the same thing.

The Christian Apologists,[1] steeped in the metaphysic of Plato and the ethics of the Stoa, seldom speak of the Kingdom of God. Their eschatology is dominated by the quest after the perfection of the individual Christian. The idea that God's *basileia* validates a claim to sovereignty over men is out of their ken. The Christian's task is to strive to be like God; he hopes for the *basileia meta theou* (Justin, Apology I, 11, 1). Athenagoras, Apology, xviii, 1, 2, conceives the *epouranios basileia* as the Creator's power over all

[1] Cf. R. Frick, op. cit. (p. 54, supra) pp. 35-45.

events—but this text stands alone in the Apologists, even in Athenagoras. Justin uses the word *basileia* chiliastically of the millenial Kingdom, not clearly distinguished from the eternal Kingdom. The Kingdom is promised as an eternal reward for the righteous, in contrast to the pains of Hell (Dialogue, cxvii. 3); in cxxxix. 5 *basileian klēronomein* is equivalent to *ta aiōnia kai aphtharta klēronomein*. But besides these unusual expressions *basileia tou theou* is often found in quotations in Justin's Apology and Dialogue. He cites the O.T. and *logia* of Jesus to make clear the relation between promise and fulfilment, and to clarify God's demands upon man. But the link with the proclamation of Jesus and his Apostles is more formal than real: the starting point is not the efficacious grace of God, but the freedom to live virtuously, coupled with the claim to reward. Thus the Apologists make a two-sided impression: on the one side Greek concepts of immortality, of (eternal) life, of attaining insight, bulk larger than the biblical *basileia tou theou*: but the words of Jesus and the Apostles, even though only quoted and not fully developed, also safeguard the Christian teaching from being metamorphosed into philosophy of religion.

This sets the stage for further developments in Church History and Dogma.[1] From the second century alongside the one-sided ethicalising of the *basileia*-concept, there was a one-sided eschatologising which expressed itself in early Christian apocalypses with their gnostic flavour, Acts of Martyrs, and above all burial inscriptions and catacomb pictures. In contrast, Clement of Alexandria sets Greek philosophy in the foreground; his *basileia*-concept is steeped in Platonism and Stoicism—he uses Stoic terms to define it (*Strom.* ii. 4, 19, 3 f.). Belief in gradual progress

[1] Cf. R. Frick, op. cit. (p. 54, supra) pp. 73ff.

(*prokopē*) displaces the biblical last judgement. Similarly, Origen's well-coined term *autobasileia* (p. 54, supra) leaves out at least part of the N.T. message of God's Kingdom. Different from this Oriental-Greek speculation is the Latin West, with its faith in the actual realisation of God's Kingdom upon earth: on this soil the development of the concept of the Kingdom of God culminates in Augustine's identification of it with the Church.

INDEX OF AUTHORS CITED